# The
# Philippine–American War

# The
# Philippine-American War

Two Personal Accounts of the Conflict
Against Philippine and Moro Forces

A Soldier in the Philippines
by Needom N. Freeman

The Battle of Bayan and Other Battles
by James Edgar Allen & John J. Reidy

LEONAUR

*The Philippine-American War: Two Personal Accounts of the Conflict Against Philippine and Moro Forces*
*A Soldier in the Philippines*
by Needom N. Freeman
*The Battle of Bayan and Other Battles*
by James Edgar Allen & John J. Reidy

Leonaur is an imprint of Oakpast Ltd

ISBN: 978-1-84677-920-6 (hardcover)
ISBN: 978-1-84677-919-0 (softcover)

**http://www.leonaur.com**

### Publisher's Notes

The views expressed in this book are not necessarily
those of the publisher.

# Contents

# A Soldier in the Philippines

Needom N. Freeman

# CHAPTER 1

# I Join the U. S. Infantry

Needom Freeman, in the United States regular army during the years 1898-1900, was born in the quiet little country village of Barrettsville, Dawson County, Ga., on the 25th of September, 1874.

Many things have been said and written of army life during the Spanish-American war, but usually from the officers' point of view. As a matter of fact the ideas of a private if spoken or written are unbelieved simply because the prestige of office was not attached, and receives but little credit.

The early part of my life was passed in and near the little village of my birth. Working on the farm and attending the village school a few months during the time when farming operations were suspended, consumed about all my time. My father being a poor man with a large family and unable to give his children the benefit of any advanced education, it fell to my lot to receive but little instruction. I was the eighth child in a family of thirteen—five sons and eight daughters.

Having attained the long awaited age of twenty-one, when most young men are buoyant and full of hope and ambition, I turned my thoughts westward, where I hoped to make my fortune. I gathered together my few possessions and proceeded to Texas, arriving at Alvarado, Texas, the second day of November, 1895.

Obtaining employment on a farm, my old occupation was resumed for eighteen weeks, but finding this too commonplace and not fulfilling my desires nor expectations, the farm work was once more given up.

I obtained a position with a wrecking crew on the Santa Fe Railroad. For twelve months I worked with this crew, then gave it up in disgust.

A few weeks' employment in the cotton mills of Dallas, Texas, were sufficient to satisfy me with that sort of work.

I next obtained employment with the street railroad of Dallas, filling the position of motorman, which I held for three months. One night, while with several friends, the subject of enlisting in the army was discussed; this strongly appealed to me, and studying the matter further, I became enthused over the idea. I determined to enlist at once. My position as motorman with the street railroad company was given up. My salary was forty-five dollars a month, as against one-third that amount in the army, but this made little difference to me. I was anxious to be a soldier and live the life of one.

I proceeded to the recruiting office in Dallas to stand an examination, was weighed, then measured all over, every scar was measured, my complexion was noted, my age, place of birth and all about my people were taken. My fingers and toes were twisted and almost pulled off. It occurred to me that possibly my examiners thought my fingers and toes might be artificial. After part of two days' weighing, measuring, finger pulling, toe-twisting and questioning I was pronounced subject and sent to the St. George Hotel, in Dallas, to await further orders. Of twelve applicants who were standing the same examination I was the only successful one. I enlisted under Lieutenant Charles Flammil for a service of three years, unless discharged before the expiration of that time. I was to obey all the orders of my superior officers, which meant every officer from corporal up.

From Dallas I was sent to Fort McIntosh, south-west of Dallas, on the border of Texas and Mexico, on the Rio Grande. My long cherished hope was now being fulfilled. I had from a mere boy had a desire to be one of Uncle Sam's soldiers and fight for my country. I had now entered the service for three years and will let the reader judge for himself whether or not he thinks that I should be satisfied with the service and experience of a soldier.

Fort McIntosh is in Laredo, Texas. Here I was assigned, upon my arrival, to Company A, Twenty-third United States Infantry. I had only been there a few days when Company A was ordered out on a practice march of one hundred and twenty miles. Of course I wanted to go, thinking it would be a picnic. I only had a few days' drilling at the fort, and that was all I ever had, but I was anxious to go on this march with my company, and Goodale, called "Grabby" by the men, had my uniform and necessary equipage issued to me and let me go with the company. I learned during the first days' march its object was not to have a picnic, but just to try us and prepare us for the service we might at any time be called upon to perform. We were to get hardened a little by this practice march.

The second day out we were halted every hour and rested ten minutes. During one of those rests I pulled off my shoes to see what was hurting my feet. I found on each of my heels a large blister and several small ones. A non-commissioned officer saw the condition of my feet and ordered me into the ambulance. I was afraid the soldiers would laugh at me for falling out. First I hesitated, but very soon I had plenty of company in the ambulance.

The march was through a rough country, the roads were very bad, and travel was difficult. Twenty miles a day through chaparral bushes and cactus is a good day's march for soldiers, with all their equipage. The infantryman carried a rifle, belt, haversack and canteen. Tents were pitched every night and guards stationed around the camp to keep away prowling Mexicans and others who would steal the provisions of the camp. Tents were struck at morning and everything put in readiness for the day's march. The company was out fifteen days on that practice march across the plains. Four days, however, were really holidays. We spent them hunting and fishing. Fish and game were plentiful. A few deer were to be found, but ducks and blue quail were the principal game. The company returned to Fort McIntosh on the third of December.

I had to be drilled as a recruit; never having had any military training, everything was new to me. I was drilled hard for a month before I was assigned to the company for duty. That month's drill was very hard.

After I was assigned for duty I learned something new about military affairs every day for a year. The manner of all the drill masters was very objectionable to me at first; I did not like the way they spoke to a soldier and gave commands, which, if disobeyed, punishment was inflicted. The month I drilled as a recruit by myself I was under Sergeant Robert Scott of my company. During that time I thought Sergeant Scott the most unkind man I had ever seen. He looked ugly and talked harshly. I thought he meant every word he said. After I learned how the commands were given and was taught how to execute them, it seemed very simple and then I was assigned for duty.

When my time came to serve on guard duty I did not understand the "general orders" and "special orders." I went on guard perfectly bewildered with the instructions given me about my duties.

I did not know what to do. I watched for the officer of the day to make his round and give orders every day and night.

Two hours' duty on post was the time we stood guard before being relieved by the proper authority. If a man is caught sitting down while on duty he is severely punished by being placed in the guard house, and sentenced to hard labour for a long time. Sometimes the labour sentence runs as high as six months or more, according to the gravity of the offense.

I was very careful not to get in the guard house or miss roll call, having to pay fines or working hard all day with a sentry over me.

Every soldier had to be on his bunk at eleven o'clock at night; his check was taken and delivered to the officer of the day. Nine o'clock was bed time, but the checks were not taken up until eleven. The first call of the morning was sounded at a quarter before six, when we must answer to reveille, followed by a drilling exercise of fifteen minutes. After breakfast every soldier had to sweep under his bunk and prepare it and himself for inspection, which took place after drill hour, which was from eight to nine o'clock.

A gymnastic drill of thirty minutes each day, except Saturday and Sunday, was given the company for a month, then for three months this was omitted, then another month's drill was given us, and then the same intermission; thus we had them alternately the whole year.

The Sabbath receives but little notice in the army. All duties went on just as any other day.

Several hours every day were unoccupied by the soldier's duties. The men could amuse themselves during these hours by reading newspapers and books, as a very good library was at hand. Aside from reading were such amusements as billiards, cards and music. These became monotonous and disgusting to me, and in less than two months I would have gladly given up my position, but I was in for three years, and had to stay and make the best of it.

# CHAPTER 2

# New Orleans

The Christmas holidays were delightful indeed for soldiers, no tasks to perform for one whole week, except guard duty. The week was spent in gambling and revelry.

All other holidays meant hard work all day for soldiers; usually they were days of celebrating some event in the history of our country or some man must be honoured, and homage paid to his memory. The soldiers on these occasions had to parade and march along the streets all day. Every holiday, except that of Christmas, was a dreaded day to soldiers.

April first, 1898, my company was ordered out on the target range for practice. We had had but little practice, only being there six days when orders were received to prepare to leave our post at a moment's notice. Those were memorable days. History was being added to, or rather made, almost daily. Every one was talking of war with Spain, its results and possibilities. Our camp was in a commotion, expecting war to be declared at once. Everything was put in readiness for marching. In this condition we remained until April seventeenth, when orders came at last for the Twenty-third to proceed to New Orleans.

The city of Laredo gave our regiment a grand banquet before we left there. Every man, woman and child, apparently, who could get out to see us off, turned out.

The Twenty-third Regiment had been stationed at Laredo for eight years, and during this time great attachment had been formed between the soldiers and citizens. From Laredo to San Antonio was a long run, attended by nothing of interest. At San Antonio the citizens demonstrated their patriotism and hospitality by having a grand banquet awaiting our arrival. Every man seemed to have a good time while there. Before our train left, the citizens put several kegs of beer in every car. This was appreciated very much, as beer seems to be a soldier's favourite beverage, and one that he will have if he has money and is where it can be bought. A soldier rarely refuses beer when offered to him.

From San Antonio a run of forty hours carried us into New Orleans on April nineteenth.

For a month we were there on guard duty. The majority of the regiment seemed to enjoy their stay in New Orleans, but for me it was anything but enjoyment.

The citizens were very kind to all soldiers, and seemed to regard them very highly; when one went into the city he was generally given all the beer he wished to drink, and made to feel welcome.

Soldiers care very little for anything, and do not seem to care very much for themselves or for each other. They know that the responsibility rests upon the officers, and that food and clothing will be furnished as long as they are in the army. When a soldier draws his pay, usually the first thing he looks for is some place to gamble and get rid of his money in a few minutes, then he can be content. He is restless as long as he has a dollar, and must gamble or take some friends to a saloon and drink it up, then go away drunk.

If one man has any money and expects to keep it he must not let others know of it, for they will expect him to spend it for all. Generally when one man has any money it is free to all, and it is enjoyed as long as it lasts. Soldiers are very generous and good-natured men; if not that way at first they become so before a service of three years expires.

Army life is dangerous to the morals of many young men. They will take up some bad habits if they have not power and determination to control themselves. It is very easy for a man, especially a young man, to take up some bad habits and lead a different life altogether in a short time after he becomes a soldier. A man soon learns to drink and to gamble, although he may have known nothing of these vices before his enlistment. I thought that a soldier's life would suit me, but after a service of three years I can truthfully state that it was not what I desired. Life in camps at one place a little while, then at another place, winter and summer, rain, sleet and snow, with twenty men in one wall tent, is very disagreeable, unhealthy and unpleasant. I spent one month in camp in New Orleans during the hot weather, and all the pleasure I had there was fighting mosquitoes. We had a fierce battle with them every night.

My regiment had all the service at New Orleans they wanted in the line of guard and special duty. Four hours of hard drilling five mornings in each week, special duty in the afternoon, then half of every night fighting mosquitoes. May was very hot. I believe that the battalion and skirmish drills, without stopping to rest or to get water, were very injurious to the soldiers.

I know that they injured my feelings very much.

I was a private in Company "A," Captain Goodale in command. I thought a great deal of my captain; he was a good officer, and was soon promoted to major of the 23rd Regiment, and commanded it for several months. He was then promoted to a lieutenant-colonel and assigned to duty with the Third Infantry, then in the Philippines. After he set out to join his new regiment I never saw him again. He was the first captain I served under.

Soldiers who served under good officers were fortunate, but if they had bad ones they were soon in trouble and had a hard service. A son of Lieutenant-Colonel Goodale, who

Troops headed for the Philippines

TROOPS ON A BARGE HEADED FOR MANILA

TROOPS OUTSIDE MANILA, 1899

PHILIPPINO TROOPS, 1899

THE RUINS OF MANILA AFTER AMERICAN SHELLING IN 1899

WOUNDED PHILIPPINOS, 1899

WOUNDED AMERICAN SOLDIERS AT SANTA MESA, 1899

PHILIPPINOS SURRENDERING IN 1900

was a lieutenant, was placed in command of Company "A." He, like his father, was a good officer, and soon won the confidence and esteem of his company.

After the declaration of war between the United States and Spain, the 23rd Regiment was recruited to its full quota of one hundred men for each of twelve companies. Four new companies had to be formed, which were called, at first, skeleton companies, because they only had a few men transferred to them from the old ones.

Non-commissioned officers were transferred to the new companies and placed in charge of the recruits, to drill and prepare them for duty.

Drilling recruits is hard work, and all the officers avoided it as much as possible. From the 20th of April to the 24th of May we had nothing but drill.

When Admiral Dewey destroyed the Spanish fleet in Manila Bay, orders were sent to the 23rd Regiment to proceed at once to San Francisco. It will be remembered that we had gone to New Orleans under orders directing our regiment to Cuba, but everything had changed so suddenly that we were ordered to San Francisco to be in readiness to go to the Philippines.

The orders from the War Department were received by Colonel French on the night of the 23rd of May.

The following day everything was put in readiness for leaving for San Francisco, but to hasten preparations all our tents were struck at 4 o'clock in the evening. Soon afterwards it commenced raining for the first time during our stay at New Orleans. Our tents were down and we had no place to shelter and pass the night. We were ready to leave next morning. I never saw so many wet soldiers before. I was on guard and saw two hundred men or more go into stables that were near our camp. We were camping in the race track of the city fair grounds, which were surrounded by a great many stables. This was rough fare, and I could not say whether the men slept or killed mosquitoes. One thing I know beyond question: I saw the toughest, sleepiest looking lot of men next morning that I had yet seen in my military service. They all seemed to have colds. To add to our discomfort all the rations had been boxed and marked for shipping, and we were without food for breakfast. Those who had any money were allowed to go out and buy something to eat. It is plain that if a man had no money he went without breakfast.

The men were all formed in line with gun, belt and knapsack, and were kept standing ready to march at the command, until one o'clock in the evening before taking up the march of three miles to the railroad station. We marched through the city and to the station without a halt. It seemed to me the hottest day I ever knew. It had been nearly twenty-four hours since I had eaten, and I think my condition was no worse than that of the whole regiment, with but very few exceptions.

We were in the city of New Orleans, and rations were plentiful, but it seemed they were scarce for us. This, however, was only the beginning of what we were to get accustomed to in a few months.

At two o'clock on the 25th day of May, our regiment boarded the cars of the Southern Pacific Railroad and set out on its journey for San Francisco. The regiment was divided into three sections for the journey, which was made in six days.

The rations issued to us on this journey consisted of hard tack, canned tomatoes, canned salmon, and last, but not least, nor more desirable, canned horse meat. To use a soldier's expression, such "grub" is almost enough to make a man sick to look at, but this made no difference, we had to eat it. I have seen a few people who seemed to think soldiers were not human beings like other people. They thought they could endure anything and would eat any kind of stuff for rations.

While eating supper one evening in our camp at New Orleans, the men were seated in their usual manner on the open ground grouped around their mess kits containing their rations; a young lady with her escort was passing through the camp and observing the men eating supper, remarked to her companion that the soldiers looked like men.

She had possibly never seen a soldier before.

At another time a man with two small boys were looking over our camp and talking about the soldiers, when one of the little boys noticing the soldiers eating, and seeming to be interested in their manner of eating, said: "Papa, will soldiers eat hay?" His youthful curiosity appeared to be fully satisfied by the father answering: "Yes, if whiskey is put on it."

Crowds of people were out at every city and town we passed through awaiting our arrival. Some had bouquets of beautiful flowers for the soldiers containing notes of kind words and wishes, and signed by the giver. Some gave us small baskets of nicely prepared rations. These were what suited us most, and were very highly appreciated by every one who was fortunate enough to get one.

Our train passed through many places without stopping. We saw crowds of people at those places with bouquets and various gifts of kindness and appreciation which they had no opportunity to give us. Whenever our train stopped it would only be for a few minutes, and there was only time enough to receive the little tokens of kindness and good will, exchange a very few words, and we would again be off.

CHAPTER 3

# To the Philippines

Travelling through western Texas and the plains of New Mexico is very mountainous and lonely. Villages of prairie dogs here and there seem to be about all the living things that the traveller sees. These little animals burrow deep in the ground, thousands of them close together, and this is why it is called a prairie dog town. I was told that these little dogs live mostly on roots and drink no water. I give this as it was told me, and do not know how true it is. One thing which I noticed was that we would travel two or three hundred miles and not see any water courses.

The section that I was with was detained about three hours at El Paso, Texas, on account of some trouble on the road ahead of us. Many of us took advantage of this to look about the city. A considerable change of temperature was noted, it being much cooler than at New Orleans. Before the next morning we were passing through New Mexico. It was cold enough to wear an overcoat, but as we only had blankets every man had one drawn close around him, and was then shivering with cold. This cold weather continued until the Rocky Mountains were crossed, and we began to descend the Pacific Slope.

Crossing the deserts of Arizona was disagreeable. The white sand from a distance looks like snow, and is so dry and light that it is lifted about by the wind. Some places it will drift several feet deep. The railroad company kept men employed all the time shovelling sand from the track. Nothing but some scattering, scrubby bushes grows in the deserts. Almost any time looking from the cars there seems to be smoke away off in the distance. This is nothing but the dry sand being blown about by the wind.

Where the railroad crossed the deserts they are from one hundred and fifty to two hundred miles wide.

The first place we stopped after crossing the Rocky Mountains was in the city of Los Angeles, California. The good people of Los Angeles had a bountiful supply of oranges and other nice fruit, which were given to the soldiers, who enjoyed them very much. Some towns where we stopped the citizens would put two or three crates of oranges in every car of our train.

The country was beautiful, orange groves and orchards of different kinds were numerous and fine.

California is the most beautiful country I have seen in my travels from Georgia to the Philippine Islands.

The Oakland Ferry was reached about ten o'clock on the morning of the first day of June. Our regiment commenced to cross at once over to San Francisco. A detail was left to take our supplies from the train and load them on boats, all the balance of the regiment going across. My first sergeant was unfriendly to me and included me in the detail as a mark of disrespect to me, although it was not my time to be placed on detail duty according to the system of rotating that duty.

Our detail worked very hard for about two hours and seeing no prospect of dinner we crossed over into San Francisco to find something to eat. We found our regiment just ready to enjoy a grand banquet prepared by the Red Cross Society. It was prepared near the piers in a long stone building; long tables were piled full of all that a crowd of hungry soldiers could wish for, excellent music was furnished while we did full justice to the feast before us. The Red Cross has spent a great deal of money since the commencement of the Spanish-American war; it has accomplished much toward softening the horrors of war by caring for the sick and wounded, providing medicines and necessaries for their relief, and doing many charitable acts too numerous to be enumerated here. Many men to-day enjoying health and strength were rescued from what must have been an untimely grave had not the work of the Red Cross come to their relief when sick or wounded. The army physician frequently was a heartless, and apparently indifferent man about the ills of his patients. While at Camp Merritt I was sick for a month. The physician pronounced the malady fever; he did not seem to care about my recovery or that of any other man; his chief concern seemed to be that of obtaining his salary of one hundred and twenty-five dollars per month. Beyond this his interest seemed to cease, and if a sick soldier recovered he was considered lucky.

There were many sick men in Camp Merritt in the months of June and July. We were stationed there for five months.

Twenty-five men, myself included, volunteered to be transferred from Company "A" to Company "E." This transfer was made on the sixth of June, and was done to fill up Company "E" to its full quota for the purpose of going to Manila on the transport Colon, which was to leave San Francisco on the fifteenth of June.

My company, now Company "E," was being prepared by Captain Pratt, and was drilling for the last time in the United States before going to Manila. I unfortunately became ill and had to be left at Camp Merritt to go over later. It was sad news to me, for I wanted to go over with this expedition.

One battalion of the 23rd Regiment was left at Camp

Merritt, which included my old company, to which I was assigned. We stayed at Camp Merritt until about the middle of August, when orders were received to go to Manila. By the time everything was packed and ready to strike tents a second order was received, not to go to Manila, but to go to Presidio, in San Francisco, and await further orders. About the 10th of October, to our great joy, orders were read out at parade in the evening, that we would start to Manila on the seventeenth. The men were so glad they threw up their hats and shouted for joy. We were glad to leave the cold, foggy and disagreeable climate of San Francisco, and delighted that we were going to Manila, which was then the central battle field.

The bad climate, incidentally mentioned, of San Francisco seemed to be only local, extending along the coast for only a few miles.

I have been in San Francisco when it was cold enough to wear an overcoat, and going across the bay to Oakland it was warm enough for a man to be comfortable in his shirt sleeves. The distance between these two points is only six miles. The native citizens of San Francisco, and those who have been residents for many years and accustomed to the damp, foggy atmosphere, are very healthy.

But this climate was very detrimental to the soldiers in Camp Merritt, and fatal to many.

While stationed in Camp Merritt I spent a great deal of time in the San Francisco park, which contained one thousand acres of land.

A great variety of wild animals and many different kinds of birds were there, and I found in it a great deal of interest and amusement. Crowds of people were there every night. Many people were there for the purpose of committing some crime. People were frequently being sandbagged and robbed, or sometimes boldly held up, and money and valuables secured.

I knew a great many soldiers who were robbed, some-times they received bruised heads just by loafing in the park at night.

No reflection is intended to be cast upon the police whose duty was in the park; there were a great many of them, but they did not know all that was being done in the park, and it was necessary for a man to keep a sharp look-out for himself if he wished to escape uninjured.

The date of our departure the Red Cross gave a fine dinner for all who were going to leave the camp. This was the custom with that society when any soldiers left there for the Philippines.

All those who left while I was there partook of a splen-did dinner just before leaving.

This society, in addition to the dinner given to us, had several hundred dollars worth of provisions put on board our transport, and all marked, "For enlisted men only on deck."

At three o'clock in the afternoon of the seventeenth day of October, 1898, we sailed on board the transport "Sena-tor." The provisions put on board for us were well cared for—by the officers, who took charge of them and guarded them so well that if an enlisted man got any of them, he had to steal them from under a guard. Actually had to steal what belonged to him by gift, and if caught stealing them he was court-martialled, and fined enough to buy his rations for a month, but the fine money was not appropriated in that way. We had a rough voyage, not on account of the weather, but because the transport was so packed and crowded that a man did well to walk from one end of the ship to the other. We were crowded like a cargo of animals bound for a slaughter pen.

A private may think all or anything he pleases, but he does not have an opportunity to say very much about any-thing. He must obey the commands of his officers.

Our officers on the transport had everything to suit

themselves, and the private had to do the best he could and try to be satisfied, or at least appear that way.

It would take two-thirds of the deck for half a dozen officers to have room. They thought themselves so superior to the privates they did not want to be near them. Our ship had fifteen hundred men on board.

We reached the port of Honolulu, after several days' sailing on rough seas, October twenty-fifth; five days were taken to coal for our long voyage to Manila. Honolulu is a fine city, about 2,190 miles from San Francisco. Located as it is, away out in the Pacific Ocean, makes it the more attractive to a Georgia soldier who was on his first sea voyage. There are some fine views in and around Honolulu. As our transport steamed into the harbour of the city I thought it a grand sight. From what I could learn I had but one objection to it as a desirable place to live—leprosy is too prevalent. A small island is used for the lepers' home, where all who are afflicted with this most loathsome of diseases are carried, yet the fact that those poor victims are in that country is a disagreeable one and makes one shudder to look at the island. No one is allowed to go there, except on business, and they have to get passes from the authorities to do so. I had no desire to visit the place.

Honolulu is a very good city, with some of the modern city improvements, such as water works, electric lights, street railroads and ice factories. These are the results of emigration, people of other countries going in with money and experience. The natives are called Kanakis. Agriculture consists in the cultivation of rice, bananas, cocoanuts and coffee. It was there where I first saw bananas, cocoanuts and coffee growing. A lieutenant, with about twenty-five men, including myself, went out about six miles along the beach. We went to the Diamond Head, six miles eastward from Honolulu. This is an old crater of an extinct volcano. Returning to the beach we went in bathing and enjoyed it very much.

Our party had to get passes and present them to guards on going out and returning. Our transport having coaled and made all the necessary preparations for the voyage to Manila, we went on board and sailed about four o'clock in the afternoon of October the thirtieth. But few of the soldiers had been sea-sick before arriving at Honolulu, but after leaving there many of them were ill for several days.

I think that the native drink called swipes was the cause of much of it. This had been very freely imbibed by the soldiers. It is a peculiar beverage, producing a drunkenness that lasted several days. Some of the men getting over a drunk on this stuff, by taking a drink of water would again be drunk. I escaped sea-sickness and, but for the fact that we were living on the transport like pigs in a crowded pen, I would have gone over comfortably and would have enjoyed the voyage.

Our rations were very poor, scarcely fit for hogs to eat. They consisted of a stewed stuff of beef scraps, called by the men "slum;" prunes, hard tack and coloured hot water for coffee. Once a week we had a change from this of salmon or cod fish. I believe those who shared this food stuff with me on this voyage will bear me out in the statement that it was tough fare.

The soldiers were not alone on board—there were other passengers who seemed to dispute our possession and waged war on us both day and night. These belligerents were known as "gray backs," some of them being nearly one-fourth of an inch long and very troublesome. Clothing and everything else seemed to be full of them.

I have seen soldiers pick them off of their bodies and clothing and kill them before the men went to bed, hoping to get rid of them and get to sleep.

I have seen several times almost the whole body of soldiers on board sick and vomiting. There was something peculiar about this sickness. Nevertheless, it was true; the men were fed on rotten prunes and fruit, which, after nearly all the supply was consumed, was found by our surgeon to be full of worms. This had been the cause of so much sickness. By refusing to eat this rotten stuff myself I was not ill.

About half way between Honolulu and Manila an active volcano was passed about four o'clock in the morning. Everybody went out on deck to see this great sight. Although it was raining at the time the men stood out in it to see this remarkable spectacle. It had the appearance of a round hill sticking out of the water, the whole top burning and falling in.

# CHAPTER 4

# Night Attack at Manila

The most interesting sight I ever beheld was in the China Sea. One evening, just before dark, when the sea was rough and black, threatening clouds were hovering over us, lightning shooting its fiery bolts across their path, and every indication pointed to one of those fearful typhoons for which the China Sea is noted. The crew had closed all the port holes and hatchways preparatory for the storm, which was believed to be fast approaching. While yet on deck with a number of soldiers, who were looking across the surface of the rough waters, there suddenly appeared in the water an object that looked like a woman; it had long hair just like a woman; the upper part of its body was like a woman, and to all appearances was a woman. It rose about half out of the water and sank back. Three times it did this and disappeared. I learned that this strange sea animal was a mermaid, and that they are seen during such stormy weather as we were then experiencing.

Another very interesting sea animal is the porpoise. It is shaped something like a fish, except the head, which looks like that of a hog. They will follow a ship in droves, swimming near the surface of the water and jumping out of the water and diving down like fish playing.

I have seen many living things in water, some of which were very interesting looking that I never heard any name for. A very strange, helpless-looking object is the star fish. They are often left by the tide on the beach and are perfectly helpless until another tide carries them back. A flying fish fell on deck of the transport and was picked up, greatly exciting our curiosity. This strange little animal never gets more than a few inches long. These fish go in schools; sometimes a school is so large that it covers half an acre or more, skipping or flying along on the surface of the water sometimes one hundred yards before striking the water again. I had in my hands the one that fell on our deck and examined it with a great deal of curiosity. It had a pair of small wings and was very beautiful.

The jelly fish does not look very clean and nice. The largest one I ever saw was eighteen inches thick and looked like a mass of jelly and was hard in the centre. These fish are of two colours, white and black. They can sting when they touch the naked body and give as much pain as the sting of a yellow jacket. I have been in the water bathing and one of them would sting me, making a great, red, burning spot. I have seen sea serpents, but was never close to one where I could see it plainly. They seem to be very easily frightened, and I only saw them on the surface of the water at some distance. They are very large snakes with black spots.

The men on our transport were interested in a flock of sea gulls, which to us appeared to be the same birds following our vessel to pick up the scraps thrown overboard. I could see them any day and I therefore believed they were the same sea gulls. They can fly farther than any other bird.

We arrived in Manila Bay November twenty-second, and anchored about two miles out from the piers of the city. The view was delightful to all on board, especially the soldiers. We were happy and jokes were freely passed around. We were once more to be on land and what person would not be happy over this thought after so long a voyage over the great waters of the Pacific?

Five days we had to wait before quarters could be obtained and we could land. I was very anxious to get away from that transport, which to me was worse than a jail. I never was jailed in my life, but I believe that two months' imprisonment would have been more pleasant than the time I was on board that ship. Finally we were landed at a point just below the Bridge of Spain and marched into the walled city of Manila. It will be remembered that a portion of the Twenty-third Regiment had preceded us a few months. Our landing would reunite the regiment, and to celebrate the occasion that portion of it that went over first had a banquet dinner prepared for our arrival. It was a memorable occasion long to be cherished by my division of the regiment. After such disgusting food as we had had since leaving San Francisco we appreciated the elegant feast and plenty of Manila wine that was set before us. This latter portion of the regiment did full justice to the occasion, both provisions and wine, which was excellent. We stayed in the city and performed guard duty for a few months. It was of the hardest sort all the time that we were in the Philippines. It was performed day and night part of the time.

We had "running guard," which was day and night, but this would not continue more than a week at one time. Manila was then a dangerous place for Americans and our guard and patrol duty was desperate work.

All the citizens of Manila were our enemies as long as the Spanish soldiers remained in the city; when they were sent back to Spain conditions improved immediately.

No one was permitted to go out of the city. The citizens were allowed, at intervals of several days, to pass out through the sally ports of the wall and take two hours' exercise in the Lunetta, which is the favourite outing grounds of Manila, and a place for executing insurgents. This was a privilege not often granted, and when the people were thus indulged they had to be back on time.

Aguinaldo, with his army, was just outside of Manila from the time the Americans captured it until his attempt to enter and capture the city from the Americans. This attempt was made on the night of February ninth, the first demonstration indicating his intentions being made about nine o'clock in the night. The Filipinos attempted to enter through the sally ports and were promptly discovered by the guards, who commanded a halt. The command was not obeyed and the guards fired upon them. This seemed to be the signal for a general engagement by the Filipinos. The Nebraska Volunteers were the first to receive the attack of the enemy. At once the battle became furious and continued for several days and nights. The enemy was making a desperate and determined effort to enter the city, but failed, and were finally driven back to a position where they could be easier handled by our forces. After about ten days' fighting the Americans threw up works and entrenched themselves and waited for re-enforcements before taking the offensive. The American forces numbered ten thousand in the city and the enemy's forces were estimated at sixty thousand. The American lines were getting too long and weak to risk an attack and we held our position and waited for re-enforcements to arrive. During this time the Filipino prisoners were closely guarded and forced to bury their dead. Five days were occupied in this work of picking up and burying the dead Filipinos. The number of their dead is unknown, but must have been large. It was reported that five hundred Filipinos were buried in one day. It was also reported that eighty Americans were killed in one night.

I shall never forget that night attack; I was one of three men on guard in the Spanish hospital. This was a very dangerous post at any time, but on an occasion like that it was more so. Three hundred Filipinos were in the hospital, about one hundred prisoners and about sixty Spanish women. All the hospital corps of attendants were armed with some kind of weapon, usually a knife. When the attack was made on the guards at the wall and the firing commenced, I was sitting in a chair and almost asleep from exhaustion and continued guard duty. A Spanish woman in the top story of the hospital heard the firing. She ran down to where I was sitting, took me by the shoulders and was shaking me vigorously when I first realized what was taking place. She was very much excited and jabbered at me in Spanish, which I had no knowledge of and did not understand one word she said. When she saw that she could not make me understand her Spanish she went away. I heard the firing and knew that an attack was being made. The Filipinos in that hospital would have met with little resistance from only three guards had they made a dash for liberty. They could have easily passed out through the unlocked doors while we could have killed a few. After gaining the outside they could have given assistance to their comrades, and in the darkness of the night set fire to the city and made our situation a desperate one indeed. The Filipinos knew the city much better than the Americans and had Aguinaldo been possessed with the nerve and ability he could have entered with his superior numbers and captured the city. The Filipinos, however, gave the Americans some hard fighting before the enemy's forces were scattered over the island of Luzon. After the Filipinos were scattered they divided into small bands, which marched over the island burning and destroying. One of the bands when run upon by the Americans would give them a short desperate fight and flee to the hills in safety. Frequently it happened that a squad of American soldiers would be outnumbered by a band of the enemy, and it was then the Americans turned to run into Manila for safety.

A great many of the native business men, both employers and employees, stayed in Manila after it was captured and carried on their business. Many of these were a menace to the safety and the authority of the Americans. All the arms and ammunition and dynamite that could be obtained by them were hidden away. They banded together to do all the mischief possible, but our guards were too clever for the Filipinos and always detected their schemes and plots before they could be carried out. It was believed that the men inside of the city were working with the enemy outside for an outbreak. Aguinaldo would engage the attention of the Americans and these treacherous Filipinos and Spaniards inside would do a great deal of mischief before being discovered.

Therefore, in the face of all this, much depended on the efficiency of our guard duty. Guards were on duty in all parts of the city, in church towers and every place that would give any advantage in keeping a lookout for any indications of trouble.

# Chapter 5

# Gunboat Expedition

Before Aguinaldo's attempt to enter Manila the friendly natives outside the city were suffering from a fatal epidemic of some character, apparently so, judging by the number of caskets taken outside. This continued for several days; one or two caskets every day were allowed to pass out by the guards, although orders were issued to search all boxes, trunks and baggage; yet these caskets were allowed to pass through un-molested for about fifteen days. Finally the guard's suspicion was aroused by these frequent burials and it was decided to open a casket, which was packed full of Mauser rifles. This ended the funerals outside. This demonstrates the trickery and smuggling schemes of these people.

I have known prisoners to escape by exchanging cloth-ing with their wives, who were permitted to visit their hus-bands in jail, the man passing out and leaving the woman in prison. A great many prisoners escaped in this way before the scheme was discovered.

Dummy guns and soldiers were placed in forts in a man-ner to deceive Americans as to the strength of the works, but the Americans were not to be bluffed so easily and this scheme was worthless.

Almost the whole American force was on the streets of Manila watching and expecting an attack for two weeks before it was made. We were always prepared to fight. We had to keep our clothes on all the time and our guns and belts by our side. I did not have more than fifteen nights' rest from the 20th of January to the 24th of May. Frequently we would just get on our bunk when a call to arms would be given; every man would rush out in a hurry and sometimes had to march four or five miles, before stopping, through rain and wind, or whatever weather we might be called out in. There we would stay the balance of the night. If we wanted to lie down we only had one blanket to put on the wet ground. Every man had to look out for himself and get the best place he could.

We would only be in a few hours from one march until orders would be received to march to some other dangerous point; it appeared that we were only marched back to the city to take a bath and change clothing, which we needed.

I believe these marches in the night or day, in the hot climate of that country, lying on the wet ground sometimes every night for two weeks, has killed more men than were ever killed by the Filipinos. Those who never died from the exposure died from the kind of rations they ate out on the lines. It has been a mystery to me how I ever reached America again. I have been through everything and have seen as hard service as any soldier in the Philippines, and have eaten as hard grub as any of them ever ate.

I believe the Twenty-third had call to arms no less than twenty-five times. Every time we thought a fight was on hand and we would see some fun with the Filipinos. Whenever we got them started to running, which most always was easily done, then the fun was on. We were sent out a great many times to guard some town from the enemy's torch.

Company "E," of the Twenty-third, was detailed to guard the first reserve hospital in Manila and was on duty ten days. The officers feared that enough of the enemy would slip through the lines to enter the hospital and commit many depredations and kill the wounded Americans, so we were detailed to guard it and walk the streets and hold up every vehicle of the Filipinos and search them for arms and ammunition. This holding up and searching gave the sentries all they wanted to do. All the time we were there on duty we could not leave without permission. We laid about in the hot sun in the day time and at night on the ground. Some of the soldiers pulled grass and made beds to sleep on the side of the streets.

The only thing to help pass the time while on this duty was to go through the hospital and look at the wounded, some with arms off, others with a leg gone, while there were men wounded in almost every imaginable way to be living. Some would get well when it looked almost impossible for them to recover. I have seen thirty to forty wounded piled in a box car and sent into Manila, where they were put on a boat and carried up the Pasig river to the hospital. They were taken from the boat and put in a cold place till the doctor puts them on the operating table and handles them like a butcher handling a beef. Almost every day women and children were brought in with burned hands and feet, the Filipinos burning every town which they thought was about to be captured, and the women and children suffered; doubtless, many were burned to death.

Fire is a dangerous resort of the Filipino. About one hundred got through the lines into Manila and made an effort to burn the city, but the promptness of the Americans saved it, only five blocks being burned. The soldiers were kept busy guarding the negroes and keeping them away from the buildings. Big stores were burning and the fire department was too poor to save them; the proprietors told the soldiers to go in and get anything they wanted.

While the fire department was doing all it could to save the city and sneaking Filipinos were hindering the department all they could by cutting the hose. They would assemble in crowds and then the hose was cut; every one caught in this act was shot down on the spot. Six or seven were thus punished that night. It was an exciting time and looked as if Manila would be burned in spite of all our efforts to save her. The Twenty-third Regiment did guard duty all night on the west side of the city. The enemy, failing to burn Manila, fired a little bamboo village outside; the bursting bamboos could be easily heard by us. The noise was just like that of guns and the Filipinos took advantage of this noise to shoot at us in the city. They would get behind the light of the burning village and when an American could be seen in the light of the burning houses in Manila he was shot at. This was kept up all night. Our great trouble was to distinguish between the noise of the bursting bamboos and the report of a Mauser rifle. The noise of bursting bamboos could be heard three and four miles, some of them not much unlike a six-inch gun, and the reports from a burning bamboo village was almost a reproduction of a battle and would last several hours.

After guarding the burning district of the city all night we returned to guard duty at the hospital. Orders were received to march to the firing line at San Pedro Macati. We marched there on the first day of March and stayed till the tenth. We were in trenches at the front; our provisions were more than half a mile at the rear and details were made out each day to bring up provisions to the men in the works. These details were fired at in going and coming by the Filipinos, but their fire was ineffective, owing to their distance from us, until the detail neared the trenches, where the distance was not so great, and it was very dangerous. Some were wounded.

A man behind the works could not get out for a few minutes' exercise without being fired at, and if he did not get under cover soon they would get him. I have seen many men shot that way; they thought the Filipinos could not shoot. I have seen some fine marksmen among them. They could do some good shooting until they became excited and fled for some place of safety.

I have seen squads of Filipinos come near our trenches and open fire on us. A squad of Americans with their arms would jump out of the trenches and start towards them and they would soon disappear like so many frightened deer. I was in a squad of soldiers who ran three Filipinos for two miles. They were shot at several times, but got away.

We were out ten days and had two engagements; we had a very hard time on this excursion. Water was hauled two miles and a half on a two-wheeled vehicle, in old vessels holding four or five gallons. By the time we could get to the kitchens about half of it would be spilled.

Buffaloes were used like oxen in this country. They were much larger, however, of a dark brown colour and very easily frightened. When one started to run away no man could hold it. I have seen them run as fast as a good horse. Their horns were of immense size and flat, considerably extended. They generally did not turn aside for smaller objects when running away. On one occasion I saw one run against a stone building, knocking himself down. He arose and ran on as fast as before. Those that run at large will get in the water where it will cover them and stand with their noses out for half a day.

The fourth day out at San Pedro Macati we had a bush skirmish and some hard fighting for about two hours.

This was my first fighting and I have to confess to being a little frightened this time, but kept my nerve on all other occasions. We ran them back from the trenches and out of sight. They were not to be seen even by the aid of field glasses any more that day. We could not estimate the number of killed, as they left none on the field.

The first sergeant of my company was slightly wounded in the chest by a spent ball, from which he recovered in a few days. I was near him and heard the bullet strike him; it almost felled him. This was the first soldier I saw wounded. The way the bullets were coming I thought every one of us would be killed, but no one was shot except the one just mentioned. Out-posts were always stationed two hundred yards or more from camp every night, or in front of our trenches, to prevent a night attack. If the enemy started through our picket lines they were fired on by the pickets, who would then rapidly fall back to our lines of trenches. This out-post duty is very important and very dangerous, especially when the sneaking Filipinos were in the community.

Many nights the Americans would be aroused from their slumbers by the enemy's attacks and efforts to surprise them, and we would lie in our trenches and fire on them till they left. The enemy would be stationed on an opposite hill and they would sometimes get very close to our out-posts, who could see them moving about and talking and hear them walking in the leaves and underbrush. Our sentinels had orders not to fire on them unless they made an attack, when the sentinels fired and got back into the trenches as quickly as possible to escape being killed by our own men.

They violated the custom of the white flag frequently. A party of six or eight would leave their lines with a white flag and advance a little and wave the flag. A party of Americans would start to meet them.

Every time the Americans stopped the Filipinos stopped. They tried to get our men as near them as possible and when they thought they could get our men no nearer they would seize their rifles, which they would have concealed behind them, and fire on our soldiers. Their scheme evidently was to kill all the officers they could, but they only succeeded in killing two, as far as came to my knowledge. After a few attempts of this kind they were fired on regardless of their white flag scheme.

While at San Pedro Macati the First Colorado Volunteers would go out and sleep all night on the hill-top. Some one was killed, or wounded, every night this was done. But few Americans were killed before the advance was made on the enemy. A strong post was taken and many Filipinos killed and captured. Ninety were captured in one little bamboo village of a dozen houses. This was the morning of March tenth. That evening orders were received to return to Manila. We had been in the trenches the greater part of the ten days at San Pedro Macati, and had two engagements, one the fourth and one the tenth of March.

We set out on the return to Manila late in the evening of March tenth. We had a march of six miles to make. A heavy rain drenched the soldiers, reaching the walled city of Manila about eleven o'clock that night.

After a few days' rest Company "E" of the Twenty-third went up the Pasig river on *cascos* to Laguna de Bay, a distance of fifty miles from Manila. This is a body of fresh water twenty miles wide and sixty miles long, and deep enough to float a large steamer.

A gun boat, which stayed there in the bay, and of the same name, was boarded by a part of our soldiers and steamed up the bay for the purpose of capturing Santa Cruz. We had to go up in front of the town in full view of the Filipinos, who saw the approach of the gun boat and left in haste for the mountains.

Our boat grounded and we had to wade out a distance of two hundred yards. The bottom of the lake was uneven and by the time land was reached we were wet from running into holes of deep water. On reaching land a line of skirmishers was formed and the town was entered without any trouble. But one Filipino was seen. He was almost frightened to death. With the aid of field glasses we could see Filipinos on the mountains. When we left they returned, but before going we burned some large buildings in which supplies were stored, mostly rice and sugar. We returned to the gunboat and *cascos* late that evening.

Captain Grant, of the gunboat, wanted to go about thirty miles up the bay from Santa Cruz. We made the run in three hours. It was a very bright moonlight night. The objective point was reached about eight o'clock. On getting very close to shore an old priest was seen on the dock waving a big white flag, which he continued to wave until we landed. Captain Pratt took an interpreter with him and learned from the old man that everything there was all right. He informed Captain Pratt that he thought the town would be bombarded if not surrendered without it. There was a fine church at this place; the town was built of bamboo. A few stores and about four hundred Filipinos were there. The Filipinos had gone to the mountains while we were landing, but returned when the old priest rang the church bell as a signal that all was well. We were preparing to sleep in their bamboo houses, but Captain Pratt, fearing some treachery, ordered us to the *cascos* and gunboat to sleep, but as we were wet and muddy large camp fires were built where we could dry and eat our salmon and hard tack before going on the boats.

We had had some hard service for four days and felt very much like sleeping, but the boats rolled and plunged until we could not sleep. We were in a dangerous place. Had all the Filipinos who came into that place that night been around they could have given us a hard fight, and possibly have killed us, but, fortunately, they did not appear to have any arms. Next morning two *cascos* were loaded with captured wood and we left this place to go down and across the lake to take another town.

Our boats were anchored two miles out and an armed detail sent out in a small launch to reconnoitre. It was found to be too strong for our forces. A strong fort and almost three thousand Filipinos were in the town. We remained in front of this place until the next morning watching for Aguinaldo's gunboats. He had four in the bay. One had been captured. Just before dark one of these gunboats was sighted coming around the point of an island. It was going into port, but seeing our boats it turned back. We made no effort to pursue this vessel, as our boat was slow of speed and night was coming on. Nothing more was seen during the night and next morning we went down the lake to the Pasig river, which is the lake's outlet. Going down the river about five miles we awaited orders from Manila.

We were out on this expedition for ten days, part of this time on the Laguna de Bay and the remainder in the Pasig river.

We had a good time after starting back towards Manila, but little to do and less to care for. While awaiting orders on the river we consumed a great deal of time hunting chickens and ducks. These were very plentiful and easily caught. We fared well on these every day for a week. We also killed all the hogs that were necessary to supply our wants, and there were plenty of them. The first ones were killed by Lieutenant Franklin, who took a rifle out one evening and was gone almost an hour. At last he returned with two fat pigs which he had shot. We expected to enjoy eating them the next morning as they had to be dressed and cooked. Next morning our hopes and expectations of a good meal were exploded by finding that the pigs were spoiled. After that we profited by that experience and always ate our hogs as soon as they could be prepared. The trouble about keeping fresh meat there was the hot, moist climate. This would soon spoil it, especially if not dressed immediately after being killed.

On the ninth day of this expedition about twenty-five men went out on a hunt for porkers. Six very good-sized ones were secured by this party, to which I belonged. Another expedition went duck hunting and bagged eighty fine ones. Great numbers of chickens were everywhere in the woods and towns. They belonged to the natives. A party of soldiers caught fifteen of these while the hogs and ducks were being secured. These three parties returned about the same time loaded with the spoils of the chase.

The cooks tried to please every one and set us at dressing our game. They cooked every hog, chicken and duck for dinner that day. There were about ninety men in this company. This was one of the last three days out on this expedition of ten days. The other seven were very rough and hard ones for us.

One night some of the men made a new arrangement about sleeping. The day had been hot and clear and the open air was desirable to sleep in where we could enjoy the full benefit of a nice cool breeze which was blowing. The deck of the gunboat we thought an ideal place to spend the night. We were very sleepy. This spot was free from mosquitoes and we were preparing for a fine rest. Captain Grant looked out on deck at our positions and said: "Boys, look out up there tonight. It rains here in this country sometimes." The sky was almost cloudless and we thought nothing of rain.

About two o'clock I awoke, thoroughly drenched, and the rain falling as fast as I ever saw it in my life. Any one who has not seen it rain in a hot country has an inadequate idea how hard a tropical rain really is. My blanket was perfectly wet and the water was standing on one side of me in a pool. It took me so by surprise that I was bewildered. Finally I decided to leave that place and seek shelter. I wrung the water out of my blanket and groped about in the inky darkness and went into the engine room, where I stayed until morning. That drenching rain seemed to affect all who were exposed to it and resulted in severe colds in every instance. The twenty-fourth of March we were about fifteen miles from Manila, up the Pasig river, awaiting orders. The Pasig river is deep and wide, large steamers being able to traverse its waters. A strong under current made swimming difficult and dangerous.

Observing some soldiers across the river at a deserted bamboo village I decided to go over to them. I set out and swam till tired. Looking back I discovered that I was about half way across the river. I swam until I was almost too exhausted to raise one hand above the other. I could not tell whether I was moving or not, except, perhaps, down stream.

I was in a critical condition, but did not give up nor get excited. Had I done so I believe that I would have drowned. I know of about twenty soldiers who were drowned while trying to swim across the Pasig river.

By struggling with all my strength I succeeded in getting across. I did not know how I could get back without swimming and I decided not to try that. I was very exhausted and rested and planned a long time. Finally I found a piece of plank and getting on that I went across all right. This experience was sufficient for me, and after that I never went into water too deep to wade.

We left our river post and went into Manila. On the way down the river we met with an accident that might have been fatal to about fifty men. A *casco* had been captured in the Laguna de Bay, and about fifty men, including myself, went on board the captured vessel and were being towed into Manila by a launch. Our vessels had to pass under the Bridge of Spain. The captured boat was too high and in attempting to pass under the bridge the whole top of the *casco* was torn off, timbers and fragments of the broken vessel were flying in every direction, and it looked as if the men could not escape these missiles. I was in the stern and thought that half of the men on deck would be knocked out into the water and possibly drowned. Quicker than it takes to tell it, I was lying on my back in a close, narrow place where there was just enough room for me to wedge into. The *casco* was being pulled to pieces against the bridge and as it went farther under the bridge the rudder beam was pushed around over me with such force that it left grooves in a piece of timber not more than an inch above my face. It was that piece of timber that saved me from being crushed to death.

After the excitement had subsided a little I found that I had been struck on one side and hurt, but only slightly. The launch tore loose from the *casco* and before it could again be fastened another accident threatened us. Several large sailing vessels lay at anchor along the river and the *casco* was about to run into them. This accident was avoided and we were landed and marched into the walled city of Manila.

CHAPTER 6

# The Battle of Maricana

Our company arrived at Manila on the night of March 24, 1899. The next night our regiment was ordered out to re-enforce the volunteers in capturing Malabon. This town was full of Filipinos, who were fighting the volunteer forces then trying to capture the town. Our forces marched to the north of the town and camped. Every soldier had to cook his own provisions, if he ate any that were cooked. The march from Manila to our camp was twelve miles. Every man carried one hundred rounds of cartridges, knapsack and his provisions. The site of our camp was on the bank of the Malabon river, which was reached at sunset. We had to cross the river before camping and the only chance was to wade or swim. Some could wade, but those who were short had to swim. We wanted to cross without getting our blankets and provisions wet, but some were more unfortunate and lost them. I tied my blanket and provisions to the bayonet fixed on my rifle and crossed with them dry, but my person suffered by the water and mud. Night had come on by the time the regiment reached the camping side of the river and guards had to be put on duty at once. Our blankets were piled up for no further service while we were out on this expedition; the men, wet and muddy, had to pass the night the best they could. There were supposed to be from 3,000 to 4,000 Filipinos near by and our

54

night camp was a hazardous one. Everything must be done with the utmost caution.

The men, wet and muddy, fought mosquitoes all night and had no rest. The Filipinos could be heard all night busily tearing up the railroad track and destroying a bridge a few hundred yards from us. They dug pits in the ground and built fires in them, over which the track rails were placed till hot enough to easily bend. Bending the rails, they thought, prevented the Americans from using them again in shipping supplies over the road. The site of our camp was a low, mucky place on the river bank, where mosquitoes literally filled the air.

That was the hardest night on me of all the nights of two years' service in the Philippine Islands. I was so sleepy and tired next morning that I could scarcely hold up my head, and my condition seemed to be no worse than that of every other soldier in the regiment. Mosquitoes had bitten me through my trousers and brought blood. Frequently I have been sleeping after a hard day's service when the mosquitoes would bite my face and the blood run out and dry up in hard drops. When I could not get water to wash off these places I would scratch them off. In some cases these bites were poisonous. I have seen soldiers with large sores, caused by scratching mosquito bites. I was cautious about poisoning during my service in the Philippines.

The morning of the 26th, about four o'clock, I saw from my post, where I had been all night, a big fire in the direction of Malabon. The Filipinos had fired the town and left it. It was our purpose to capture the place and take some forts on the river, but the tricky Filipinos preferred burning their town to surrendering it to the hated Americans.

Our forces took up the advance on the enemy, who stubbornly resisted us from ten o'clock in the morning until four in the evening, when they retired to Malinto and took another stand behind a stone wall and held this position until driven from it by a charge. We had to advance up a long slope of open ground for one and a half miles. Firing was kept up rapidly all the way. The enemy was driven out and the town taken. About thirty men were killed and wounded on the American side. The enemy's loss was not known, but must have been very heavy.

One poor fellow who was among the wounded in this battle I remember very distinctly. He was first sergeant of Company G, Twenty-second Regiment. He was shot through the head. The doctor dressing the wounds as he came to the wounded saw this sergeant and said there was no use to do anything for him, that he would die in a few minutes. The wounded man replied that he would live longer than the doctor would and wanted his wounds dressed. He lay there and talked to his comrades, who were around him, and cursed the doctor for neglecting him. He remained in this condition an hour or two and died.

After a short rest in Malinto we marched about one mile south and back to Malinto again. That night we marched to a point near a station on the Manita and Dagupan Railroad and camped. We were then about eight miles from Manila, and opposite Malabon, which is off the railroad and on the beach near the mouth of the Malabon river. Our camp was located more than two miles from where we had left our blankets that morning on going into battle. A detail of ten men, including myself, was made out to go after the blankets. They were obtained and we returned to camp with them about ten o'clock that night. We had to cook our rations for supper after our return, but being rather a frugal meal of easy preparation but little time was required to prepare it; frying some bacon in mess kits composed all the cooking; hard tack and canned tomatoes composed the remainder of the meal. The ground with the starry heavens overhead and one blanket was both house and bed. The next day we marched into Manila, arriving about twelve o'clock. We remained there doing guard duty till the 30th day of March.

In the evening of the 29th orders were read out to provide three days' rations, fill our canteens and each man to be furnished with one hundred and fifty cartridges. We all expected a battle and were anxious for it, but did not know where we were most likely to get it. Every one was busy and anxious to be marching, especially the officers, who usually could hardly wait for the time to come after receiving orders to march.

We were to have supper on this occasion at five o'clock, but all we had were some scraps and crumbs from the camp kitchen.

Our orders were to march to Maricana, which was held by the enemy. We marched twelve miles before camping. It rained before we started out from Manila and cleared up, but left the roads very muddy and made marching very hard. The twelve miles were made by ten o'clock. That night the wet ground served as couch and one blanket as all the covering. We had to recline, if we lay down at all, with gun and belt at our side, ready at a moment's notice to meet the enemy's attack should they swoop down upon us in camp. After a halt of six hours we set about at four o'clock preparing breakfast, every man cooking his own rations in camp kit and making coffee in a quart cup.

Men were gathered around their little fires of wet wood on the damp ground trying to burn wet wood and cook over the little fire it made. Some of the hungry men had just succeeded in getting their fires to burn and commenced to cook when orders were given to prepare for the march to Maricana, which we were expected to capture that day and to take the Filipinos prisoners or drive them into the neighbouring mountains. It is needless to say that those men who failed to get their breakfast were ready to fight. They had an opportunity before many hours passed.

From the camp it was five miles to Maricana. The march began at four-thirty, while it was still dark, and we could move unseen by any of the enemy who chanced to be lurking in our vicinity. We marched through the woods and without speaking above a whisper marched close to the enemy before we were discovered. Their sentinels in the church towers were the first to discover our approach and give the alarm by ringing the bells.

Maricana is located on the bank of a river and we advanced within one hundred and fifty yards of the opposite bank before we were discovered. We advanced at double time and reached the river bank, when we lay down and opened fire just as the early daylight was appearing. Our skirmish line covered the whole town, in which the enemy were stationed as a reserve force to their advanced lines along the river. This advance, or outer line of the enemy, were fortified behind a stone wall. Our line was at the disadvantage of being in the open ground. The lines thus formed were hotly engaged for some time when the command was given to cross the river and charge the enemy's lines. The river bank in front of me was about ten feet high, but this offered no obstacle to me when bullets were falling thick and fast near by. At the command to cross I jumped and somehow got down the bank and into the water. Looking back I saw no one else coming. The bullets were coming around me so fast I had no time to form any plans and I pushed on into the water until it was almost over my head. I remained in this condition until I saw my command crossing about one hundred yards below me. I could not get out on the bank to go down and decided I would wade down to the crossing place and join our forces there. I was almost exhausted when I reached the shore. The enemy, seeing our intentions to attack their line, remained behind the stone wall and fired at us until we were nearly across. Then they could stay there no longer and fled from their strong position. We crossed and entered the town, capturing five armed men. The enemy beat a hasty retreat, rather a pell-mell flight across the open country towards the mountains, at whose bay they had entrenchments and a large reserve force. The fight lasted from daylight till about two o'clock in the evening. The battle of Maricana was as hard as any fought in the Philippine Islands. About three thousand American soldiers were engaged. Several were killed and a great many of the Filipinos.

When an American was wounded his wound was dressed and some soldier's blue shirt hung up near him to designate the place where a wounded American was. In this way no one would be left on the field after the battle when the dead and wounded were picked up.

The Filipinos were not so well cared for. I saw a great many soldiers run out of their way in order to step on a dead or wounded Filipino. They would shout with joy at their punishment of the poor Filipino.

I was near three Americans who were shot that day; two of them were killed. The one who recovered was a member of my company. A ball passed through his body, entering the back and passing out on the right side. It didn't seem possible for him to live, but in one month he was again at his post of duty. A lieutenant of the Fourth Infantry had his horse killed under him. Jumping off he took out his field glasses and got on his knees and began looking for sharpshooters. In less than a minute he was shot through the heart and fell dead without speaking. I thought every second I would get a bullet, for they were flying so thick and close that I did not see how I could escape them. Before the battle was over I wished I might be shot, for I never was so nearly dead in all my life. My condition did not appear to be any worse than that of every other American soldier.

We were run almost to exhaustion and were awfully hot. I drank water that day from ditches and holes when the water looked green and tasted very badly. I knew the water was filthy and even dangerous to drink, but I was not going to die for water when there was plenty of it near by. During the heat of the battle I was lying down near an old soldier. We were both trying to get cover. We were fighting hard with no protection but the ridges in a large rice field which we were fighting over. Our firing line was in a line of skirmishers. A bullet hit the ground in front and between the old soldier and where I lay. It knocked dirt in our faces. The old soldier looked at me and appeared to be very much frightened. I only laughed at his funny looks. Before I got away from that position I felt a hard shock on my chest. I thought that I was shot at last and put my hand up to examine the wound. Finding myself all right I looked at the ridge and saw what it all meant. A bullet was buried in the ridge. I dug it out with my bayonet and kept it, and I have it yet as a souvenir of that day's battle. I have several more bullets which struck near me at different times and places. All of these I treasure, for I do not expect to get any more bullets just as I did these.

The American loss at Maricana was twenty-four killed and nineteen wounded.

# CHAPTER 7

# Night March to Caloocan

After leaving the battlefield we returned to the camp we had left that morning. The whole force was almost exhausted by the day's service and marching was a slow, burdensome task. A great many men lost their provisions in the battle or in crossing the river. Mine was lost in the river together with my mess kit, canteen and haversack. Those who were fortunate enough not to lose their rations of canned beef and hard tack were enjoying a hasty meal. At this juncture orders from Manila were to march to Caloocan Church that night, a distance of about twenty-three miles. It was then getting late in the evening and this march to be made before camping was not very pleasant news to already footsore and tired soldiers. Before marching out of sight of our camp men began falling out. I marched about half an hour and had to fall out of ranks and straggle along as best I could. My company set out for Caloocan with one hundred and twenty-eight men, only eighteen of whom marched through that night. The others were scattered along the route, footsore and worn out. Many of them pulled off their shoes to relieve their blistered feet and marched barefooted and carried their shoes in their hands, and, like myself, stopping almost every hundred yards to rest a few minutes. We were afraid to stop long at a time. We would have become too sore and stiff to move.

We continued to move along in this tedious, toilsome way as rapidly as possible. My party of three were proceeding as best we could. In the darkness of the night we lost our way by taking the wrong road and went into a small town, where we found a few white men, one of them a doctor belonging to the First Regiment of Colorado Volunteers. He made many inquiries about us and our regiment and asked all about the battle fought that day. He looked after our welfare by providing us with shelter and beds, but there was something else we wanted before sleeping. We were perishing for food and all we had between us was a small can of bacon, a ten cent United States coin and one small Spanish coin (a *paseado*). With these we went out to buy bread. We found a Chinaman and bought a piece of bread that was so hard we could scarcely eat it, but we made a very good meal on that and the bacon.

We slept on a good spring bed and I awoke next morning in the position I was in when I fell asleep. I was so stiff and sore that it was miserable to have to move. After breakfast we went into Manila and took the railroad for our command.

A number of soldiers arrived after we did and reported for duty. All the provisions that I ate on this expedition, which lasted three days, would not have made more than one good meal. Before my party reported at Caloocan one of the other two and myself were reported captured by the Filipinos, or lost. That night we all went back into Manila to resume guard and patrol duty. Police duty was all done by soldiers until a force of Macabees was organized. The Macabees are enemies of the Filipinos, and soon became our allies and were very good soldiers and police.

Manila has a population of nearly 400,000 people of different tribes and nationalities. It is the capital of Luzon and the most important city of the Philippine Islands. The energy and enterprise is due to foreigners. There are several miles of narrow gauge street railroad and a system of electric lights.

To mingle with these people it is necessary to know two or three languages, if not more. Spanish is the prevailing language. Most of the business men can speak several languages.

The Chinese are the filthiest people there. I have seen hundreds of them living in their workhouses where a stench was arising too great for a white man to approach. These filthy people cook, eat and sleep all in this filthy hole. Their principal food is rice and soup. One dollar of United States currency will buy enough for one person to live on a whole month. When the Americans first entered Manila it was very filthy. The air reeked from the accumulation of filth during the siege of the city. This made the place a little worse than usual. It took the soldiers three months to clean out and clear out the streets.

The only thing apparently that kept down a great deal of disease and death is the continual blowing of the sea breeze.

Those killed in battle outside the city had been carried in and buried in shallow holes, or probably I would be more correct in saying, about half covered with earth and left that way for dogs to scratch up and pull about by the arms and legs.

I have seen dead Filipinos carried out of the hospital, thrown on carts and carried to the burying ground and handled like dead hogs. They would be covered a little and left to the dogs. I don't believe I ever looked towards the place without seeing dogs there eating and pulling the bodies about.

Hundreds of beggars are to be seen squatted down at all public places and on the street corners. They do not sit down like Americans. This is the case with all the natives. They sit in a peculiar, squatting way, which is positively tiring to any one else but these natives.

The Filipino men wear trousers rolled up high and a long white shirt of very thin material, the tail hanging out over the trousers like a sweater. They wear nothing on the feet and most of them wear nothing on the head. They are not fond of clothing, and many wear very little, almost going nude. They find a great deal of pleasure in the possession of a gun and it seems that they are content with a gun, fighting and running in the mountains. They care little for life and will fight till killed.

A squad of Filipinos was captured near Manila by some of the Fourteenth Infantry; when they were approached to give over their guns to the soldiers they would make a motion like giving up a gun, but instead jump back and attempt to shoot a soldier. If he succeeded in shooting an American some other American would shoot the Filipino. Several were killed in this manner.

When a Filipino is captured his greatest desire is to keep possession of his gun, and sometimes fight for its possession after being captured.

The Filipinos are a natural race of gamblers; they gamble and trade, many of them, for a living, refusing to work as long as they can get anything to eat without working for it. Their principal cause for idleness is the cheapness of their living, rice and fish being their principal food. They will catch fish and throw them in the hot sun for two or three days; they are then taken up and smoked and burned a few minutes over some coals and chunks, and then eaten.

If any Americans are watching them they will say, *"mucho chico wino,"* while eating this delicacy of their indolence and filth. The Filipinos and native tribes are extremely filthy in their eating, as well as everything else; they eat almost anything that an American will refuse to eat.

The Macabees is another negro tribe on the Island of Luzon. They are a much better people than the Filipinos and more intelligent. This tribe is hostile to the Filipinos, and fight them whenever an opportunity is offered.

Two regiments of the Macabees were organized and equipped by the Americans, and placed in the field against the Filipinos, and they made very good soldiers.

The 20th Kansas advancing

The 20th Kansas in action

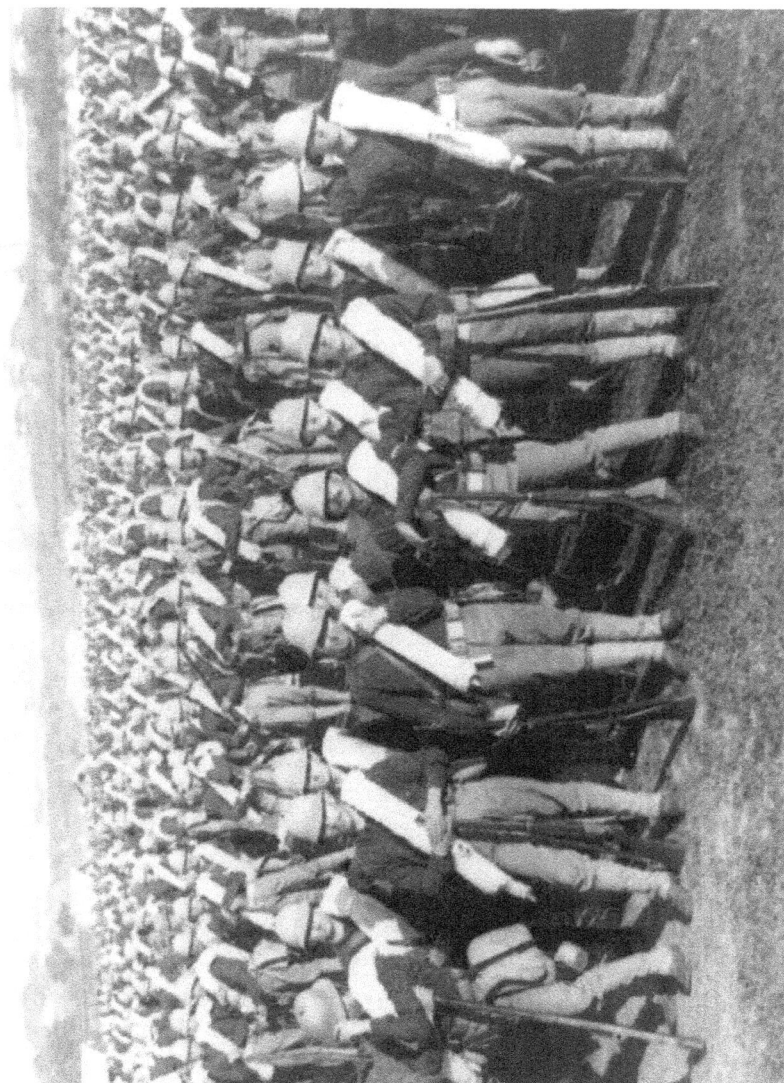

The 38th US Infantry in tropical service hats

AMERICAN TROOPS IN ACTION

A WOUNDED AMERICAN SOLDIER BEING TREATED

SOLDIERS OF THE 35TH U.S. VOLUNTEER INFANTRY ADMINISTERING THE "WATER CURE"

# CHAPTER 8

# The Dredger Guard

I missed being placed on a detail of twenty-five men to serve on a gunboat; I wished to get out on some kind of service and leave the regular and dull service in Manila. I missed this detail in all probability by being out in the town when the detail was being made out. I tried to get on when I returned, but failed, the detail having been made out already. This detail from my company saw much more service than those remaining in the company.

Their discharges show a record of more than a dozen engagements. They served in this detail five months, and had plenty of hard service. They were only paid once during the five months; a few of them, however, were not paid until discharged, if I was correctly informed. Their descriptive list was lost, causing two men to have to serve ten days longer than they enlisted to serve.

Much "kicking" was done by men in other parts of the service who were not paid for a year or more, but all to no purpose.

I was on the alert for another detail to be made and to get on. At last I succeeded, on the tenth day of April, in getting on a detail of only ten men to perform guard duty on a dredge boat that was dredging at the mouth of the Malabon river. This was twenty miles from Manila. The object of the dredging was to make a channel in the shallow water at the river's mouth sufficient to enable gun boats to enter the river, which was deeper after leaving its mouth. This was very slow work, requiring a great deal of time and labour to perform it. This dredging had been going on for a month. We were on duty there for ten days, and, judging by what I saw, it must have required two months' more work to open the desired channel.

From our station numbers of natives could be seen on shore, and passing up and down the river. It seemed that the country was full of Filipinos.

We watched them a great deal. Their methods of catching fish was very interesting to us. They never used a pole, hook and line as we would. At night great crowds could be seen, each one in a boat, and carrying a big torch. They would be near the beach, going out but a little way from the edge of the water; they would beat and splash in the water, and drive the fish into large traps or nets, just like a hunter driving quail into a net, only the fishermen were more noisy.

After beating the water and banks until it was supposed the fish had gone into the net, or trap, they were left in it until next day, when they were seined out. Great quantities were caught in this way.

Another method of fishing was to get in a boat with a long gig and move the boat slowly, and when a fish was near enough gig it. The large fine fish were only caught in this way.

Our detail returned to Manila in the evening of April tenth, and remained there until that portion of the 23rd Regiment was ordered to the Island of Jolo, where we started on the seventeenth day of May. I had been in the old walled city of Manila a little more than six months; part of my regiment had been there ten months. We had had very hard service there, and the close confinement, almost like imprisonment, made us glad to change, and held out a hope that we would find easier service and more interesting.

The wall of the old city of Manila extended entirely around the old city. The sally ports and all the streets were always guarded until no soldier could go outside without exhibiting a pass to the guards signed by the company and commanding officers. All the time that I was stationed there I was never out without the required pass.

Guards were stationed on top of the wall, and made it unsafe to try to climb it to get out, although I have seen this done by means of a rope; men would pass out this way and stay out as late as they wished to and return.

This was not safe. Even the guards did not discover the attempt, for the wall was not less than thirty feet high, some places even higher, and forty feet wide. Stone houses are built in this wall, and used for military stores. On top of the wall on the sea-side were three hundred large cannon when the city was surrendered to the Americans. Around the old Spanish arsenal about two acres were covered with cannon balls, guns, bayonets and rifles, all scattered about in a mass until it was difficult to get over the ground. It required two months of the American's time to pile up and arrange these munitions of war surrendered by the Spanish.

After the treaty of peace all these were returned to Spain.

A great many Spaniards live in Manila, and are subjects of Spain. They have some very peculiar customs. One that came to my notice is that of the courtship of a Spanish youth and his sweetheart. The young man is not permitted to enter his sweetheart's home, but stands on the outside and makes love to her though the iron bars of a window. I saw a great deal of this before I learned what it all meant.

The Spanish seemed to have a very bitter hatred for all Americans just after the fall of Manila. When we first entered the city the Spanish women would throw anything that menaced us in passing the streets, from their windows. They would do anything to harass and endanger the lives of Americans that they could think of without exposing themselves too much. Starvation was staring them in the face when the city was surrendered. They had been reduced to rice almost wholly for sustenance. The pay of the Spanish soldiers was very small. I was informed that it was only six dollars Spanish per month, equivalent to only three dollars of United States currency. Yet this meagre sum had not been paid for several months.

A Spaniard is not a very frank, attractive looking fellow to an American soldier. He has a sneaking countenance, and a disposition out of harmony with that of the American. However, this opinion may be modified somewhat with those able to speak Spanish and become better acquainted with them. Being unable to speak their language I was barred from this possibility.

Luzon and some other large islands are very fertile, and under proper agricultural management would yield millions and blossom as the rose, but as yet they are blighted by the uncivilized natives. A man would be taking his life in his hands to go out into the country and try to engage in anything. As conditions existed when I was there, bands of hostile Filipinos were scouring the whole interior, and frequently were bold enough to raid near the American posts, leaving devastation wherever they went. The soil is very fertile, a warm temperature and plenty of water to irrigate with if desired for that purpose.

The natives use the most crude implements, and have but very little knowledge of farming, and are too indolent to put into practice what little they do know of soils and crops. It seems to make little difference what season they plant in. The climate is always warm, most of the year extremely hot; too hot for an American or white man, to labour in. It is just the climate that suits the negro. Chinese and negroes work for fifty and sixty cents per day.

A very fine tobacco is raised, and most of it exported. A cigar factory in Manila manufactures a great quantity of cigars.

Rice is easily raised, and is the principal food of the natives. The rough rice is husked in a very crude way; a wooden trough, or dug out, is used to put the rough rice in, and chunks of wood are taken in the hands, and the rice is pounded with these until the husks are all broken off, the rice taken out and separated from the husks.

Sugar is an important crop, and is extensively raised. No less than fifteen sugar mills could be counted from the top of the walls of the city of Manila. Under improved methods of agriculture that country would be a wonderful one in the production of sugar and rice.

The Philippines will, in all probability, become important in the near future in the production of minerals, principally gold. There are some very good veins of gold ore in the mountains of Luzon, some of which I saw myself. Several pieces of stone on which gold was easily seen, were picked up by the men of my regiment. I saw rocks with both gold and silver in them. The men would not tell just where they had found them. They probably thought that at some time, after their service expired, they would return and work the places found.

I knew one man, an old, experienced miner, who would spend the Sundays out in the hills and around the foot of them, where he was not exposed too much to the enemy, prospecting for gold. He was successful in finding good indications of rich minerals. He appeared to make a confidant of me. At one time he showed me a lot of gold and some silver that he had found out on his prospecting tours, but would not tell me where they came from. He told me that when he was discharged he intended to return and work the mines. I knew that the paymaster had considerable money belonging to this old miner, who told me he should invest it in the mines, and in purchasing mining machinery.

I saw and heard enough to cause me to believe that

when the natives are civilized, and when men would be safe in the mountains, that the mines in the Philippines will attract more people than the Klondike ever did. There are advantages in the Philippines which are not found in the Klondike region, the most important being the climate, not considering the quality of the mines, which I believe to be equal to that of the Klondike.

The mountain regions are rich in various minerals.

In the Island of Mindanao coal has been mined ever since Americans have been there.

This country will find out in a few years what is in the Philippines. I believe it is a rich country. Almost anything can be raised that is desired in the line of field and garden crops; fine timber is plentiful and saw mills are yet unknown. I don't believe there is a saw mill in the Island of Luzon. All sawed timber is imported that is used at present; not much is used in building as most of the houses are built of stone or bamboo. The frame buildings which we have in America are never seen there. All the native houses and small towns are built of bamboo, and covered with grass. The bamboo grows very large, the joints are two and three feet long, and some of the larger bamboos are as large as a common tree. They are the same thing that people in this country know as canes, the difference being in their size only. Houses are built of bamboo without the use of nails. Nothing for flooring but the naked earth. Split bamboo is worked into the houses fastening the whole together. I have seen the natives build houses, and have no other tool than a large knife. The roof of grass is fastened on with strips of bamboo, and is three to four inches thick. This roof is superior, in point of comfort, in a hot country, to that of anything I ever saw. I have been in the hot sun and in metal roofed buildings, and on going into a grass covered house the difference was noticeable immediately, the grass roofed house being much cooler.

Manila is built of stone; the buildings look very old, but are good yet.

One night when the Thirteenth Minnesota Regiment was on police duty, and no one was allowed on the streets after seven o'clock at night, with a fellow soldier I started out to go to a dance outside of the city walls; we knew that if we were caught we would be court-martialled. To avoid all the risk possible we went out before seven o'clock, and took chances on getting back to quarters safely. We could not return to our quarters without passing sentinels, that much was certain, but how to pass them safely was the question then most important to us. I had an army pistol, and with that in my hand I directed my friend to play the part of a prisoner and march before me. We proceeded in that way only a short distance when a guard halted us. I explained that I had a prisoner carrying him to headquarters. The guards were to see orders for a pass or whatever orders I might have, but this one allowed me to pass on with my prisoner without showing any orders. We passed in by all the guards and patrols on the streets, and were halted and some questions asked and answered, but none of them asked to see any orders regarding my prisoner, who all the time was just in front of me. I was afraid that every guard and patrol would demand my orders, and then our scheme would fail, and we would be in trouble. I told them it was late and I must hurry in with my prisoner, and so we passed them all and reached our quarters in safety. The men worked a great many schemes to get out and in, but it was for my friend and myself to play the part of prisoner and guard first.

I never tried any more schemes on the guards, but was always in at night; I did not like to risk so much just for a little fun. We were very careful about keeping our little scheme from the officers, but told some of our comrades about it, and enjoyed the joke with them.

# CHAPTER 9

# The Moros

On the seventeenth day of May the Thirteenth Regiment and two battalions of the 23rd Regiment went on board the Spanish transport, "*Leon*," and sailed for the Island of Jolo.

I was a member of one of the battalions of the 23rd. We boarded the "*Leon*" under a Spanish crew and sailed under the Spanish flag. The "*Leon*" was a large vessel of rapid speed, and made the run from Manila to the Island of Jolo in a little more than forty-eight hours, a distance of 800 miles south of Manila. Land was in sight almost the entire voyage. We passed through straits and seas, by Iloilo on the Island of Panay, Cebu, Negros Island, through the sea of Jolo to Zamboanga on the Island of Mindanao, and to Jolo. The group of islands forming the Sulu Archipelago is the southern islands of the Philippines. The "*Leon*" sailed into the Jolo Bay in the evening on the nineteenth of May. A large force of Spanish soldiers was stationed in the town performing garrison duty. Our force was to relieve them, and they were to return to Spain on the transport "*Leon*." On the twentieth of May we went ashore. The Spanish soldiers seemed to be very glad to be relieved and return to Spain.

The garrison was short of rations, and the soldiers were living very hard when we relieved them. These Spanish soldiers were the last who left the Philippines for Spain.

We were landed in small boats, which could not carry very many men. The boats were rowed by Chinese. All supplies have to be carried in by these small boats. It is a very slow and tedious piece of work to land the contents of a large ship, and requires several days to do the work.

Captain Pratt was in command, and Company E was ordered out to the block house, which stands about one thousand yards back of Jolo, and towards the mountains. A guard detail was made out, and the Spanish soldiers were relieved. I relieved the first Spanish of his post at Jolo. When I approached him he began to speak in Spanish and tried to make me understand what, I supposed, were his orders he was turning over to me. I could not understand him, and told him to go. Of course I had enough orders without his, if that was what he was trying to explain to me.

The Spanish went to work with a rush getting everything ready to leave. They had been there for a long time. I learned that the commanding officer, who was an old man, had been there twenty-eight years. In the evening at two o'clock the Spanish flag on the block house was hauled down by the Spanish soldiers and the Americans unfurled to the breeze the Stars and Stripes. The Spanish seemed to be very much grieved, the officers wept; the Americans were jubilant. Everything passed into our hands, and the various responsibilities of the place with all its dangers also passed to us. The natives, who belong to the Moro tribe, are treacherous. We knew nothing about them and their intentions. Guards were put on duty at once, six being around the block house so that a Moro could not get in if the attempt were made to enter it, and thus made it a place of security to our troops. The Moros a few years ago massacred more than one hundred Spanish soldiers in the block house Astora. It was a cruel and treacherous piece of cunning of savage barbarians. The Moros had been warring against the authority of Spain, and causing the Spanish troops much trouble. At last apparently tired of rebelling, the Moros agreed to make peace with the Spanish. According to an ancient custom of the Moros, when making peace with an enemy they would give pearls or some other gift to their enemy. The captain of that Moro company was going to make peace, according to this custom, and taking some fine pearls and a body guard of one hundred of his men he entered the enclosure where the Spanish soldiers were lined up in two columns with unloaded arms to receive them. The Moro captain and his body guard marched between these lines, and as the guard neared the Spanish captain the Moro advanced with his pearls, and getting near the Spaniard instead of giving him the pearls he quickly drew his sword and dealt the Spanish captain a death blow. The Moros, who understood the prearranged treachery, opened fire on the Spaniards, who were helpless with unloaded guns, and the entire garrison of more than one hundred men was massacred except one man, who, in the noise and consternation, succeeded in crawling into a sewer pipe, and through it into a big stream of water, and escaped without injury. The Moros gave the Spanish a great deal of trouble, probably as much as any other tribe of the Philippines. The Moros have a bad record. I believe that I had rather fight the other tribes than the Moros; they are more treacherous than other tribes. They go armed all the time with the *bolo*, a large knife carried in a wooden scabbard. From the oldest man down to little boys, they all carry the *bolo* or a big knife. I have seen old men, so feeble they could scarcely walk, carrying a fine *bolo*. They will not part with them day or night, but keep them as their only friend, refusing to let any one take them from their hands to merely look at them. These arms are very fine, and range in cost from five to fifty dollars. They are manufactured of the very finest steel, the handle of many of them is made of silver and finely engraved. The edge is kept very sharp. The blow of this dangerous weapon is generally enough to kill a man. I was informed that a Moro never struck his enemy but two blows with his *bolo*, one on each side; if that did not disable him the Moro would run for his life.

A steel armour is worn by a few of them, to furnish protection to their bodies. But most of the tribe would rather risk their life than wear anything, even clothing. Only a piece of cloth is worn around the waist and loins. In this piece of cloth is carried a box containing a stuff to chew called *beadle* nut. Only the married men are allowed to use this, as they have a law prohibiting its use by the single men. It is a soft green nut growing on a tree which looks very much like a hickory tree. A piece of the nut is placed on a leaf, which is always carried in the chewing box, and some salve is also placed on the leaf, then the piece of nut and the salve is rolled up in the leaf, and the chew is ready for use. The married men can be very easily distinguished from the unmarried ones simply by the use of this, which makes the chewer's mouth as red as red paint and the teeth black. The teeth of the single men are very white, but just as soon as one marries he begins chewing *beadle* nuts, making his mouth red and teeth black in a few days. Their marriage customs are not exactly like ours in America. A Moro can marry a woman, or buy one for a price ranging from fifty dollars up to one hundred and twenty-five dollars. After marrying a woman or buying one, if she doesn't suit her husband he doesn't have to wait for a court to set aside the marriage, but can simply let her go and proceed to get another in the same manner.

The men are prohibited from having a plurality of wives at one time, but are allowed to have just as many as they desire, simply getting rid of one and then getting another.

The women wear big legged trousers, which only reach down to the knees. Sometimes women are seen with more clothes on, but they look as if they were torn almost off.

The clothing of both men and women is worn out before they ever change. A few who lived in the towns wore more clothing than those in the country. The men wore pants which seemed to cling to the skin, they were so tight. Those in town were no cleaner than outsiders. They get so filthy and slick that an American can smell one as far almost as he can see. The more clothes a Moro wears the filthier he is. Those wearing no clothing, except the girdle around the loins, are the less filthy. Nothing is worn on the head and feet.

Leprosy is a common malady, as well as numerous other diseases of the skin. All of which doubtless arises from the filthy habits of the people. Doby itch is very common. It is a very bad skin disease, and hard to cure when it gets a firm hold, and will have fatal results in a few years in that warm climate. One doctor said that it would require three or four years' careful treatment to cure an acute case of doby itch in another climate.

Almost every day I saw a bad case of it. The legs will become swollen, and large knots and tumours cover them until walking is extremely painful. It is easy to contract doby itch. About two weeks after I reached Manila the first time, I discovered a small sore spot on my leg, which looked like ringworm. I was informed that it was doby itch, and that I should have it doctored before it spread. I began to treat it, and it itched seemingly to the bone, and began to scatter. I would wake at night scratching and clawing the itching spot, and lie awake for two and three hours. I had to trim my finger nails closely to keep from ruining my leg scratching it. It continued this way for several days before I checked it. Many of our soldiers had a similar experience, some of them much worse than mine. I guarded against it afterward, using all the precaution I could to avoid it. A friend of mine who enlisted when I did, caught a severe case of the doby itch which kept him in an almost help-

AMERICAN SOLDIERS AT AN OUTPOST

AMERICAN SOLDIERS ON PANAY ISLAND, 1899

Defending a blockhouse in Manila

A BURIAL DETAIL FOR ENEMY DEAD

less condition for eight months. He was finally discharged for disability, a wreck for life, without anything but a small pension of about eight dollars per month.

To the Moros again. There is a class whose religious teaching is that when one of them kills seven white men he will go to a better country when he dies. He thus makes sure of his entrance to what is heaven in their religious belief. The Americans soon learned to distinguish one of this class, and watched them very closely. One of them will not wait for much of a chance to kill a white man, but will make his chance to do his deadly work. I have seen a great many of them, and know that they attempted to kill our men on duty as out-posts. They would not have any guns and would go to the walls of the fort and try to scale them to get to the Americans and kill them with *bolos*. Without trying to kill them the soldiers would shoot towards them to drive them away.

When one of their number dies the grave is dug one day and early the following morning the funeral begins. Every one carries something to eat, a big bottle full of *beno* (a native beverage) and a bottle of whiskey. Four men carry the corpse on two small poles, all the others fall in behind in column of twos and then they proceed to the grave-yard, drinking their beverage and enjoying themselves. The crowd stays at the graveyard all day, and drink and carouse until they are well filled with liquor, and all get drunk. This is the program every time one of them is buried. It is a big picnic for them.

Once a year regularly they prepare some of the best rations they have and carry them to the graves and leave them there through the night, believing that these are enjoyed by the dead. I learned that this was an ancient custom of theirs, having been learned probably from the Chinese.

The Moros seem not to care for anything, not even for life. A large number, probably two-thirds, never had any home. They did not know where they would go, and seemed not to care.

Some of the islands had two or more tribes of negroes, who would have a governor to each tribe and make laws for themselves. If natives of one tribe crossed the line into the territory of another and stole fruits, cocoanuts, of anything else, and the injured tribe could catch the thief or thieves, their heads were cut off and their bodies left on the spot. This is according to their laws. Beheading for theft, and leaving the bodies where they were beheaded. I have seen five or six in this condition two or three times.

One tribe would sometimes array itself against another for battle and fight till great numbers of them were killed. Our troops stopped several such battles by going out where they commenced to fight. As soon as we would arrive they would stop fighting, and there seemed to be an end of the trouble between them. They appeared to be in great fear of our guns. They have a few old rusty guns, which are only used to fight enemies of other countries; never using them to fight each other with. When General Bates made a treaty of peace with the Sultan of Jolo, the sultan was received by General Bates the first Sunday in May, 1900; we were drawn up in line and presented arms to His Excellency. The sultan was to maintain peace on the island of Jolo, for which he was to receive 500 dollars Mexican coin every month. We presented arms to him, and were forced to treat him with great honours. I can assure the reader that for myself it would have been more pleasant to have gone out to meet him on the battlefield, and when I speak thus I feel safe to make the assertion that many more were of the same disposition.

After these formalities were over I had opportunity of examining the guns of the sultan's body guard, also the ammunition. The guns were so rusty that I would have considered it safer to be shot at by one of them than to shoot the gun. The barrels were almost closed with rust.

A lot of the bullets were wrapped with cloth, and stuck in the shells. Some of the bullets were loose, and some were driven in very tight. All of the shells had the appearance of being in use a long time, and that they had been fired as many times as they would stand.

A man was taking his life in his hands to go out into the country alone. Many people have been killed in this way. There is a tribe that would cut off a man's head for amusement, or to see how it looks.

Guards were kept on duty all the time, and no American was permitted to go outside of the wall without having a pass. This was kept up for a long time after we went to Jolo, and was then restricted to one thousand yards from the fort, and no less than four men together. The Moros gave us very little trouble, doubtless the result of extreme caution. They never had an opportunity of making any demonstration, so it is uncertain what they would have attempted had the opportunity been given them. They are too treacherous to be trusted about anything whatever.

They have very little knowledge of firearms; probably the only guns they ever had, and also those of the sultan's body guard, were old, worn-out guns given or sold to them by the Spanish. With our improved rifles I believe that one man could withstand the attack of twenty of them armed with bolos, that is to say, were the American in some fortification, and opened fire on the Moros when they came in his range. They, of course, would not fight in this way, their method being one of sneaking treachery. They slip up behind the unsuspecting victim and behead him with their *bolo*.

I was anxious for them to engage the Americans in a fight. I desired to know something more of their methods, but they seemed not to care to fight us. They are a wandering people, seemingly with no definite purpose. As night suits their sneaking better than open day time they do as much travelling, or more, in the night than in the day time.

They could be seen on the hills around Jolo with torches moving about all night. When we first went to Jolo and saw these torches at night we thought they were signals, and close watch was kept on their movements.

They evidently made some preparations for resisting us at first, and stored away such arms as they could obtain, for later I saw twenty-eight new Mauser rifles hidden in an abandoned house on the beach. Another soldier and I secured a pass and went, at the risk of our lives, beyond the limit of our pass, and on this outing discovered the hidden Mausers. We went up the beach about fifteen miles, and went into two towns where there were a great many Moros. We watched their movements very closely, and kept at some distance from them, and never bothered anything or any one. They watched us very closely, and acted to us very strangely, but made no effort to get near us. We were a little frightened and thought it safer to get away from them, when we started on our return, the nearest and quickest route that we could. Our pistols were no doubt the instrument of keeping them away from us, and at the same time tempted them to kill us to secure them.

Some of the soldiers were afterwards killed, and their guns and cartridges taken. It was very dangerous for two or three men to be out in the woods away from any help. In the mountains of Jolo and Mindanao are wild cannibals, who would kill and eat a white man should he be found in their midst. We were not allowed to go out in the mountains, but the places where we were prohibited from going by orders of the commanders were the places most desirable of all for us to slip out and go to. The dangers to us by going out were only fascinating rather than hindering.

It was my belief while there that the natives were gathering up and storing away arms and ammunition preparatory for resisting the Americans when they thought the proper opportunity was offered. The guns I saw hidden in the house on the beach, and many other things, led me to this belief. They claimed to have some big guns posted back in the mountain. Whether this was true or not I am unable to say, for we never went to ascertain the correctness of the story. While stationed at Jolo a vessel arrived loaded with ammunition for the sultan. It was discovered and taken into custody by the custom house guards.

CHAPTER 10

# Moro Murder

All the larger islands have an abundance of game, wild hogs, chickens and deer. Wild dogs are plentiful in the woods. They are very wild, running off almost at sight of a man. At night they seem to be bolder and come around the outside wall and howl so much that people are kept awake all night.

A detail was sent out by our commander's orders to lie in hiding and shoot them when they approached near enough. We could see them away off during the day in the grass, but could not get to shoot them. The only chance for that was to hide at night and wait for them. We frequently went out and killed a number of nice fat wild hogs and carried them in and feasted while they lasted. These animals were very wild, like the dogs. A man on the ground could not get near enough for a good shot—they would discover him and run. We would climb a tree and wait for them.

The town of Siasse, on Tai Tai Island, was the station of Company H for three months. Moros almost swarmed on the island. The captain of the company permitted a squad of men every few days to go hog hunting when the supply of meat began to get short. Some of the Moros were trusted by the soldiers and were allowed frequently to go out with the soldiers on a hog hunt, as these trusted ones were thought to be harmless. One day the captain sent out five men early in the morning to hunt hogs. They hunted until tired in the evening, when four of them sat down to rest and play a few games of cards, while the fifth went to the beach near by and bathed his feet.

A crowd of Moros, twenty or more, gathered around the players to see the game. The soldiers were not afraid of them doing any mischief, as the Moros appeared friendly and quiet. As the game progressed and became more interesting the players became less conscious of their position, and those standing around.

To be more comfortable and have better use of their bodies and limbs their belts were taken off and laid by them with their guns. The Moros gathered around the soldiers saw the opportunity for mischief and seized upon it at once. They seized the soldiers' guns and belts, while six of them drew their *bolos* and began their deadly work. The first soldier who was struck with a *bolo* had his head cut off at one blow. The soldiers were making a desperate fight for life against what seemed no chance for success. Two soldiers were killed in the fight, another grabbed for his gun; getting hold of it he received a heavy blow on the head with a club, was cut dangerously in the neck, but succeeded in securing his gun so that he could fire it. The firing frightened the Moros, who commenced running. The soldier on the beach ran back where he left his comrades when he heard the shooting, but the Moros were then out of sight. Two soldiers lay on the ground dead, another was cut so much that he bled to death before they could get him back to camp, while the one who did the shooting had a terrible wound in his neck and had received a heavy blow on the head.

It was a long way to camp, and one boat with room enough for two oarsmen. Night was almost on, and the situation was perilous in the extreme. The man who was not in the fight carried the dead and wounded men to the little boat, and set out for camp as rapidly as possible. As above stated one more died while being carried to camp, making three dead and another with his head almost half off. The sea was a little rough, and only one man rowing, with a feeble help of the wounded man with one hand, made slow progress.

Camp was reached at three o'clock next morning. The wounded man recovered but could not turn his head; when he looked around he had to turn his whole body, and was discharged from the service for disability. He draws a pension of thirty-six dollars per month. Next day after the Moros killed and wounded the hunting party, sixty men were sent out to capture the murderers. The chief of the Moros was offered a large reward for capturing them and turning them over to the Americans. The Moro chief captured them, turned them over to the Americans, who then failed to pay the reward as previously promised. Six Moros were all that were guilty; these were bound together, carried out of camp and shot.

# CHAPTER 11

# Jolo to Japan

Seassa is situated ninety miles south of Jolo. Few of the men liked to be on duty there. At first entrance of our troops they had to go into camp, as there were no barracks. Barracks were built later at Seassa and Buangior by the soldiers stationed at these places. The captains of those companies were mean and cruel to their men, and worked them very hard. Some men were almost killed by the hard work at these barracks and in the swamps cutting timbers for their construction. Some while at work in the swamps had mud slashed in their eyes and almost put out. The mud poisoned them. Some had their feet poisoned by the black mud. The captains made the soldiers do the work, instead of hiring natives, and kept the money appropriated for this work and used it for their own benefit.

A soldier had no opportunity to report such frauds. If he wrote to the department commander to report anything without the permission of his immediate commander he would be court-martialled. And of course an officer guilty of such conduct was not generous enough to permit a private to report his conduct to a superior officer, and thus the privates were ill treated by some unscrupulous officers.

The hardships of the service were greatly increased or diminished according to the honesty and unrightness of the officers in command. A private is only a tool in the hands of his officers, and can be managed just as they please as long as the private remains in the service. I always thought it better to obey all orders, agreeable or disagreeable, and serve out my time of enlistment and get a good discharge, and then be free and independent. I enlisted merely to get the experience of army life, and to know just what the service really is. I found out to my satisfaction all about the army that I cared to know. The army is all right when its officers are all right. But many of them fall far short of the standard—officers who will not give a private justice as he should.

A few soldiers deserted the army. I cannot blame a man much for it. Some had good cause. But to desert the army in the Philippines and attempt to get away from the islands is almost impossible. Any one leaving there must have a passport to present when they attempt to go on board any vessel, and then if the passports are not properly executed they cannot go on board.

I know of a few soldiers trying to get away, but the farthest point they reached was Hong Kong. They would be caught very easily.

The one who reached Hong Kong was apprehended by English officers and returned to Manila and delivered to the American authorities.

One man who enlisted in Manila was discovered to be a spy for the Filipinos, securing all the information possible for the advantage of the Filipinos, and conveying it to them at every opportunity. This spy had gone with a company to which he was assigned, to Bungio for duty. While at Bungio he induced two other soldiers to desert their company and go with him to the Filipinos, promising each a commission in the Filipino army. He was an officer in the Filipino army, and a very dangerous man, resorting to all kinds of schemes and treachery to accomplish his purposes. Having persuaded two soldiers to go with him they seized a small Moro boat, and with their rifles and a good supply of ammunition they set out in the darkness of the night headed for the island of Mindanao. Ninety miles of water lay before them and their small boat. They encountered a rough sea, lost their bearings, and finally the boat capsized, and they lost their clothing and one gun after a battle with the sea for three days. Instead of reaching Mindanao they drifted on the Island of Jolo, about twenty miles from the town of Jolo, almost starved to death. In preparing for their trip they had not thought as much about rations as about ammunition. They fell into the hands of the Moros, who carried them to Jolo and delivered them to the Americans, who placed them in prison. Two of the poor fellows' feet were blistered all over by marching over the hot sands, having lost their shoes when the boat capsized. These two were unable to walk for some time. They were tried and sentenced to terms of imprisonment from five to six years. This was the common fate of all who tried to desert the army and get away.

I was on duty on several islands and in many towns in the Philippines, but Jolo suited me better for service as a soldier than any other place I was in. I was on duty in Jolo for thirteen months, and know a great deal about the place. Most all the soldiers who did service there liked it. Sailors enjoyed their visits to Jolo. Quite a number of sailors told me that they had been in a great many towns of the tropical countries, but that they would rather live in Jolo than any of them. The most undesirable feature of the town is that there are no pleasure retreats except to go to the mountains and among the Moros, and besides, we soldiers were confined very closely within the walls and on duty. The town is very small. A man can walk all through in less than an hour.

I have known of recruits on going into Jolo express their delight at the idea of doing duty in such a fine place, and wish they could stay there the three years of service for which they had enlisted. But in less than two months, seeing the same things every day, they wanted to get away, and would have given anything for an opportunity to go to another post. Everything became monotonous, and seemed somehow to be wrong.

This seemed to be the common experience of all. The town is beautifully laid out with broad streets, which are set with beautiful shade trees that are green winter and summer. A person can walk all over town the hottest days and be in the shade all the time. Three small, but very nice parks with beautiful and delightfully fragrant flowers and shrubbery lend a charm to the town.

I have been walking out in the town at night, and would smell the sweet odours from the parks for two or three blocks away. This was not occasionally so, but all the time. The soldiers enjoyed sitting in the parks and on the piers at night, taking in the cool sea breeze after a hot day. I have seen as many as three and four hundred soldiers sitting out on the piers before going into quarters.

As in all other parts of the Philippines, chicken fighting is a favourite sport in Jolo. Outside of the city wall is built a grand stand and pit for chicken fighting. It is all enclosed, and ten cents (Mexican) admission is charged unless you have a chicken to enter. Some fine chickens are entered in these fights, and a great deal of money is put up on them. Gambling is not prohibited, and chicken fighting is engaged in every Saturday all day long. The natives will gamble away the last cent they possess before they will stop. A suburban town of Jolo is Buss Buss, nearly half as large as Jolo, and built out over the water on bamboo poles driven into the mud, and left projecting above the water. The houses are then built on these poles.

Buss Buss is built over shallow water, running out over the water for one hundred and fifty yards. The houses are all built of bamboo. This seems to be a Chinese town. Many

Chinese live there and engage in business in Jolo. Chinese are engaged in various kinds of business in Jolo, but all live in Buss Buss. The Chinese and Moros are not friendly, and it is probably due to this fact alone that caused Buss Buss to be built.

Major Sweet was in command of the post at Jolo for some time. He would not allow more than one hundred Moros inside the city walls at one time for fear of trouble with them. The Moros supplied our forces with vegetables, fish and fruit, which they brought in and sold to us. To prevent the town from filling up with Moros a strong guard was stationed at the gate, which was closed at six in the evening and opened at six o'clock in the morning. The Moros would be crowded around the outside of the gate every morning waiting for it to be opened to go in and dispose of their produce. Frequently there would be twice as many as were allowed inside at one time. When the gate was opened they would rush for it, but not more than one hundred were allowed to pass inside. When one disposed of his produce, etc., and returned to the gate he was allowed to pass out, and another from the outside could pass in, and so on until all had been in and passed back.

Not far from Jolo, out towards the foot of the mountains, is a coffee field. There are several others on the island besides that one. In these coffee fields a great many Moros work all the time gathering and cleaning coffee, etc. The method is like all others of theirs, very rude and poor. They dig out long troughs of wood and place them in running streams in such a way that the water will run in at one end and out at the other. Into these troughs the unhusked coffee is poured, and then it is tramped under the feet of the cleaners until the husks are all broken off and float away with the water. The coffee is then taken out and sacked and dried out for shipping. This is the only method I ever saw in use for coffee cleaning.

Tropical fruit is everywhere abundant. The bread fruit tree grows in Jolo to a great size. The fruit is about the size of a cocoanut, except it is of a flattened shape. It is covered by a thin soft hull easily cut open with an ordinary pocket knife. The first time that I ever saw the fruit I ate half of one. I thought it as good as anything I ever ate. I believe it will alone sustain life. Cocoanuts and bananas grow in profusion. Cocoanuts are cut and dried, then exported. Oil is manufactured of the dried cocoanuts, which is of excellent quality. We used it to oil our rifles all the time we were stationed in the Philippines. Chinese and natives caught quantities of fish, which were cut up and exposed to the sun several days to dry. The fish get almost black in this process of drying and smell badly before they are dry enough to be sacked and shipped. I saw a great deal of this business, but never learned where it was shipped to or what use was made of it.

Hemp is produced from a native plant growing wild in the forests, and looks something like the banana plant. It is baled and exported in great quantities. Natives bring in small bundles of it from the mountains. Red pepper grows abundantly in the woods on the high and dry lands. It grows on a small bush, which is loaded with the pods, which are very strong.

The natives in all the islands make a beverage of the dew which collects in the cocoanut buds. This dew and water stands in the buds and is collected early in the day. It is called tuba, and is liked by all the soldiers. I drank but little of it. I saw soldiers get drunk on it, and be crazy for a week. It is like all other beverages of the islands, but little is necessary to make a man drunk.

About twice every month we went out on a practice march for one day, only leaving about one company on guard. Every man would carry his dinner, and have almost a picnic, enjoying it much more than at other times

AMERICAN TROOPS IN ACTION

AMERICAN SOLDIERS AND PHILIPPINO WOMEN

Tending a wounded soldier

AMERICAN TROOPS IN ACTION

AMERICAN SOLDIERS FORDING A RIVER

THE WAR ENDED IN 1901 WITH THE CAPTURE OF EMILIO AGUINALDO'S, HE'S SHOWN HERE BOARDING THE USS *VICKSBURG*

and places, when we would be marched out in double time several miles and have a hard fight. We went out on these practice marches up the beach and returned across the mountains, stopping to rest frequently and gathering and eating cocoanuts. If any Moros were around we would give one a cent of Mexican money to climb the trees and get cocoanuts for us. The trees are hard to climb, but a Moro seems to climb them very easily. He will tie a piece of hemp just above his ankles and go right up a tree by jumps until the top is reached. Having secured the cocoanuts we would cut a hole in them and drink the icy water in them. This water is very nice and cold, and is particularly so to hot and tired soldiers.

When we would start out on what was a practice march most of the men would think we were going out to fight, and would not know differently until we returned, for it was generally known only to the officers where we were going or what the object of the march was. Sometimes we would have a long, hard march, and always through the woods and forests, for there were no roads. In the forest marches we frequently chased monkeys, of which the forests were full. We saw more monkeys in Jolo than in any other island we were on. Sometimes when three or four monkeys would discover us they would make a great noise, and, jumping from one tree to another, keep in one direction, and all the monkeys within my hearing would join in the procession, and keep up the noise and jumping. The trees would appear to be full of monkeys over us, all jumping in the same direction, and making a great noise. We amused ourselves and added to their trouble by throwing stones at them until they passed out of our line of march, which was frequently half an hour. The wild ones are hard to catch. Young ones, too young to climb well, were easily caught, and some were captured for pets.

Natives would catch them and sell them to the soldiers.

The Sultan of Jolo was fortified about ten miles across the mountains from Jolo. He lived in his fort with his army. My last practice march was made for the purpose of viewing the sultan's position, and to know something about his forces if we had to fight them. It was about ten o'clock on the morning of the 13th of May, 1900, when our commanding officer in great haste issued orders to get ready at once. We all thought we were going to fight that time. We were formed into a battalion as hastily as possible, under the commander's orders, who was present on his charger, and directing everything. We were soon moving out to no one seemed to know where, except our commander. No dinner was taken with us this time, only guns and as much ammunition as we could carry. We marched about five miles before halting for rest. It was very hot, and several soldiers fell out overcome by the heat. Some doubtless fell out to avoid a battle, as they thought. Two men just before me, whom I knew were great cowards, and who feared that we were going into a battle, decided that they could not face an enemy. I heard them talking about falling out ten or fifteen minutes. Their minds were made up to fall out and avoid fighting; one said that he would fall out if the other would stop to take care of him. This suited them exactly, and out they went, and were left behind. Our march was continued until we crossed the top of the mountain, and from the other side we could see the sultan's fort and trenches below us. It was then about three o'clock. We rested and looked at the sultan's fort, and looked over his position carefully. This was the object of the commander in marching us out there. He was expecting to have to fight the sultan, and decided that we should see his location and know as much as possible the conditions we would have to meet in fighting his forces. Returning we arrived in Jolo in the night.

Our commander expected the sultan to attack our position, and wished to know just what to expect of us, and how quickly we could get into position to defend the fort. To ascertain this, and also to keep us in practice, a call to arms was given every month, when every man would get out and string around to the port holes in a very few minutes. Every soldier went as if he expected to have to fight. There were five companies of the Twenty-Third Regiment in Jolo while I was on duty there. Besides these one company was stationed in the Astoria block house, one company at Seassa and one at Buanga. These companies did not have as hard duty as the companies in Jolo, but every three months a company was sent to relieve one of these posts, and the relieved company would come into Jolo, where it could have the same duty and drill that the other companies had in Jolo. The companies at each of the three places just mentioned were relieved every three months.

Company E, of which I was a member, went to the Astoria block house about two months before we left Jolo and the Philippines. My company was doing guard duty at the block house when orders were received for recalling one battalion of the Twenty-Third Regiment, called the depot battalion, made up of sick men and those with less than six months' more service under their time of enlisting.

Those who had less than six months to serve were given the opportunity to stay or to return to the United States. I was not slow to accept the chance to return and was truly glad of the opportunity.

The transport Warren came to Jolo for the battalion on June 15th. The transport had come by the Island of Negros and Cebu, and took on board a battalion of soldiers who were going to return to the United States.

The "depot battalion" was made up of sick men and those who had short times. It was several days before we left Jolo. The men who were going as sick and disabled were examined by the physician. Those he believed could not endure the climate long and be able for duty, he recommended to be returned to the United States, and those who could endure the climate and proved to be healthy, stayed, unless they were of the class of short-time soldiers.

A man could not stand the climate of the Philippines many years unless he was very healthy and acquainted with tropical climates.

I do not believe the Philippines are a white man's country. I have heard doctors tell soldiers that if they stayed there, that five or six years would be as long as they could live.

Two friends and I had decided that when we served out our time that we would return to the United States by another route than that taken in going over, and thus make the trip around the world. We would go through the Mediterranean Sea to London and then to New York. But when the orders came that we could return on the government's time, and by a different route, we decided at once that we had seen enough of the world, and that the route taken by the transport would be long enough for us, and satisfy our thirst for travel.

The soldiers who had been taken on board from the islands of Negros and Cebu landed at Jolo, and went into camp, where they remained for eight days awaiting preparations of the soldiers at Jolo.

I was transferred from Company E to Company K on June 18th, and with those who were returning to the United States went into camp outside of the wall of Jolo in a cocoanut grove, where we stayed till the twenty-third day of June, when we boarded the transport *Warren* and sailed for Manila. Manila was reached on the morning of the twenty-sixth of June, where we stayed until the first day of July. A great many soldiers were added on at Manila, many wounded men and fifteen dead soldiers were put on to carry back to the United States, where the dead were sent to their relatives for burial.

While waiting a few days for all preparations to be made

I obtained a pass and entered the city for the last time and viewed everything that was so familiar to me when on duty there.

It was during this short stop of only a few days that we heard of the trouble in China.

Three regiments of United States troops were immediately ordered to China: the Sixth, Ninth and Fourteenth Infantry then at Manila. The Ninth Infantry went on board the transport *Hancock*, which was lying alongside our transport, the *Warren*, and sailed just before us on its way to China.

A rumour was circulated that our transport was sailing to China, and that we were going there for service. A great many very foolishly believed the report.

July first the *Warren* sailed from Manila bound for San Francisco. The first day out from Manila, late in the evening when supper was eaten, I ate very heartily, and went on duty in the stern of the transport. The sea was rough, and gave the transport a rolling motion. Shortly after going on duty my head commenced swimming, and I was ill. A soldier told me that I was sea-sick. I had never been sea-sick and knew nothing about how a person felt. At last I vomited freely, and in less than an hour I was all right, except the swimming sensation of my head, which lasted a while longer. This little experience was all that I had in going over to the Philippines and returning to the United States.

The fourth day from Manila we arrived at Nagasaki, Japan. The following morning the transport was ready for inspection, the crew having worked most all night preparing for it. Every man on board and everything had to be inspected before we were allowed to enter the harbour. Nagasaki has a fine, deep harbour, where steamers and war vessels coal and take on supplies. Many large ships are in the harbour at all times.

The bay leading into the harbour is between hills which

are almost entitled to the name of mountains. It is apparently a hilly and rough country to the traveller entering the bay to Nagasaki. On the left-hand side of the bay on entering is a large marble monument standing on the side of the hill. This is a monument in memory of Japan's first king. Of course I did not read the inscription, it being in Japanese; but the monument can be seen at a great distance. I learned about it from a resident of Nagasaki. While in Nagasaki I also learned that the Japanese are the hardest working, or rather the most industrious people, and receive the least compensation for their work of any race of people. Ten to fifteen cents per day is the regular price of labour. Several hundred are constantly employed in coaling vessels that enter the harbour. The coaling is done in a peculiar way. A line of men pass baskets filled with coal from one to another while the empty baskets are passed back to the place of filling by a line of children standing close enough to reach out one way and get a basket and pass it on to the next one standing on the other side; thus a continuous chain of baskets is kept going until the vessel is sufficiently coaled: the filled baskets going one way and the empty ones in the opposite direction. Men, women and children all work. Apparently no one is idle.

The lot of woman is extremely hard. A mother will fasten her child to her back and work all day with it there; sometimes it is asleep and sometimes it is yelling, but it is all the same to her. Children there do not receive the attention they get in America, but are handled roughly, and soon have to work, beginning work almost as soon as they can walk.

Hundreds of small boats, large enough to carry two or three people, are always ready to carry passengers to and from the ships and the landing for ten cents (Mexican). They are not allowed to charge more.

These small boats are provided with sides and a roof like a small house, into which passengers can go and close the door.

When you get ashore there are hundreds of little ve-hicles called *jinrikishas*, which look something like baby carriages with only one seat and an umbrella. The Japs will come trooping around jabbering to you to ride. You get in one and a Jap will get between a small pair of shafts and trot away with you, and go that way as long as you want him to for ten cents an hour. The traveller can go anywhere he desires in one of these vehicles. They do not use hacks and vehicles as Americans do. I never saw but one horse in Nagasaki. It was working to a dray, and was almost worked to death. The Jap's back seems to be his most convenient method, and almost the only one he has, of carrying anything.

Another soldier and I walked through the city looking at everything we could see. We soon discovered that almost every one was poking fun at us, all because we were walking instead of riding in *jinrikishas*. It seems that everybody there rides in them everywhere they go, and it appears funny to them to see anyone walking the streets. Peddlers are the exceptions, it seems, to this rule. A great many peddlers are seen walking the streets to vend their wares, and they have a great many articles that cannot be bought in America.

Every Japanese house has a rug or carpet on the floor—these are very nice articles. The funniest thing of all is the custom of stopping everybody at the door and have them take off their shoes before entering the house. They will not allow any one to enter their houses without pulling off his shoes. The reason of this, to my mind, is the fact that the rugs and carpets are made from grass and are very heavy, and catch dirt very easily.

# CHAPTER 12

# Back to the United States

The Japanese are industrious, good natured and friendly people. They treat every one kindly, and every one invited us to go into his house and chat awhile. Our greatest difficulty was to understand them. They appeared to be anxious to do anything they could for us, and considering everything as I could see it in our short stay, I believe I would like to live among them.

A great many Europeans are residents of Nagasaki. It is a fine town, a great deal of business is done there. The city is spread out along the bay back of the city, and all around the bay, except the entrance to it, are large hills, and on these a great many large guns are mounted. These natural barriers enable the Japanese to make the city a strongly fortified place. The government of Japan is good. Laws are rigid and strictly enforced. Theft is regarded as a very grave crime, and is punished with severe penalties.

Men with whom I talked in Nagasaki seemed to desire to leave the impression that Japan was well prepared for war, in fact better prepared than most any other country.

The transport *Warren* sailed from Nagasaki July ninth for San Francisco, taking the northern route of the Pacific Ocean. This route is claimed to be about two thousand miles longer than the southern route over which we sailed in going to Manila. The ocean currents and winds make a great deal of difference in which route a vessel is sailing in, and the northern and southern routes give the advantage to the vessels. Ships go the southern route from San Francisco to Manila and return the northern route.

After a few days out from Nagasaki we found colder water, which continued most of the way to San Francisco, only getting warmer a short distance from San Francisco. After getting out into this cold water the temperature of the atmosphere also fell, and every man who had an overcoat or even a heavy uniform put it on. Those who had only the thin uniforms called khaki worn in the Philippines, suffered from cold. It was cold and disagreeable for all on board except the officers, who, as usual, fared well at all times and in all places. There was a casual detachment of discharged soldiers numbering one hundred and thirty-eight on board, two hundred and forty-one officers and privates of the Twenty-third Regiment, sixty prisoners and twenty-one passengers, a total of four hundred and sixty men on board besides the crew. The transport *Warren* is a large vessel, and all on board had plenty of room.

Those men who were not thoughtful enough to start back to the United States with their heavy uniforms looked somewhat pitiful crowding around the engine rooms and boilers, and getting anywhere that offered some protection from the chilly air and sea breeze. I was fortunate in not being one of that number. I had plenty of warm clothing and fared well returning. I was on the lookout for myself, and provided myself with everything I desired, and had to call on no one for anything. My rule was to look out for myself all the time I was in the army, and usually I had everything I desired. If I wanted anything to use I always went where I could buy it, and never borrowed from the soldiers.

I always thought that was a good rule for a soldier; I noticed that those who did that fared much better than those who did not practice that rule.

I never liked to loan my gun and belt to a soldier when he has all those things of his own. But some soldiers would keep their guns polished and oiled, and set them away and borrow guns and belts from other soldiers to do guard duty with. These received the appellation of "orderly buckers" by their comrades, and were too lazy to walk post and perform a soldier's duty. Duty on the transport in returning to the United States was very hard on those soldiers who were well. Almost every soldier was on the sick report, and called by the soldiers the sick battalion. The few who were put on duty had it to perform every other night. I was one of the latter, and I considered it pretty tough too. Cooks on the transports were assigned for one year to cook for the soldiers. They were as filthy as hogs with everything they cooked. They cared nothing about how the rations were prepared nor how nasty they were, just so the cooking was over with as quickly as possible. They had no sympathy; anything seemed to the cooks good enough if it did not poison him. On our return we had plenty to eat if it had been cooked decently so that men could eat it. The reader may say that it should have been reported to the officer in command. This was done, and reported also to the officer of the day, and the next day after the reports were made we were given cabbage for dinner, and every man founds big worms in his plate of cabbage. While the officer of the day was passing by one soldier had the nerve to show him what was on his plate; immediately the officer of the day went to the cooks about it and that seemed to end it. One soldier found something in his plate that looked almost like a tarantula.

Some of the officers and a great many privates had a monkey apiece. Great care was taken of them by their owners. Two large monkeys belonged to some of the crew. These and the smaller ones had the whole vessel to run through and nothing escaped them—they were into everything. Finally the commanding officer gave orders for all the monkeys to be taken up, but the order was not carried out and he had the doctor chloroform the two large ones and throw them overboard. That made the crew very mad and sounded the death knell to all the monkeys on board.

That night the crew very quietly caught every monkey and threw them overboard—not one escaped. It was then the officers' turn to be mad and they did everything they could to learn who destroyed their monkeys. One old captain who had lost a monkey offered a reward of ten dollars to know who threw his monkey overboard, but he failed to find out who it was. I never heard such a fuss about as small a thing as a monkey before.

We arrived within one or two miles of the Golden Gate on July 30. The transport stopped and the whistle was blown for the quarantine officers and a pilot. We could not see land, the fog was so heavy, until we got to the Golden Gate. The sight of land sent a thrill of gladness through every one on board, especially the soldiers who were beholding their own country, where they were soon to be discharged, and once more be free to go and come at their own pleasure. Just before night we went to the quarantine station on Angel Island and remained until morning, when everything was taken off the transport. On the first of August we went ashore at the Presidio wharf, landing in the evening.

We were not received as royally as we had departed, no big reception was awaiting us, although I am quite sure the soldiers would have enjoyed one as much as when they were departing for the Philippines. I suppose it was thought that when we went away that we would never get back.

When we boarded the transport for the Philippines several thousand enthusiastic people witnessed our departure and a great display of patriotism was manifested. When that portion which returned when I did were landing only one woman and a little boy were present to show any feeling of rejoicing that we had not all perished in the Philippines from the awful climate and the Filipino bullets. This great patriotic display being over we went into camps at Presidio and remained there to rest and await further orders, which came in a few days, as soon as arrangements for transportation over the railroad could be made; and then Companies I and L went to Fort Douglas, Salt Lake City, Companies K and M were assigned to Fort D.A. Russell, Cheyenne, Wyoming. August sixth we left San Francisco and arrived at Fort D.A. Russell in the evening of August ninth. Companies K and M were under the command of Captain Delair, who is a good officer. Captain Devore had command of Company K, to which I then belonged and I remained with that company until discharged.

Captain Devore was a very good old religious kind of an officer, very strange and different from any other officer. The most that he believed in was to keep clean. He was very fond of seeing brooms, mops, picks and shovels in use. He liked to see work going on. He seemed to be too economical to eat as much as he needed of government rations. He would never allow any of the company's funds to be spent for any purpose, but was all the time adding to the fund.

The company was allowed twenty pounds of sugar every ten days. Of this Captain Devore would take off one pound for company funds. This is only one example, or illustration, of many ways of adding something to the funds of the company.

The company cook was preparing prunes one day for dinner when the old captain came around inspecting everything; the cook told him that he was cooking prunes. The cook was then asked how the men liked them, to which he was answered that the men would eat all that were being cooked and then not have more than half enough. The old captain said there were too many for the company—that six was enough for anyone. He further said, "I don't eat but two or three and that is as many as I want."

The company was always kicking about him. He was never pleased on inspection to find something cooking. He liked to find the stove cold and the cooking vessels all clean, then everything with him was O.K. He would give a man who had had a number of summary court-martials an "excellent" discharge and some soldiers who were good duty soldiers and never had a court martial would get "only good." I have noticed that if he likes a soldier he will always get "excellent." He seemed never to be governed by a soldier's record. I had "very good," all I cared for, as I was so happy to get it.

I left the army November 11, 1900, en route to Dallas, Texas, where I remained a few days and went to Pleasant Point, where I spent several days with two of my brothers, John H. and Juney H. Freeman. Here I met many friends whom I had known before enlisting in the army and again I was free to join them in their sports as I had done before.

December twentieth, I started back to Georgia. I took the route via New Orleans, at which place I stopped about thirty hours and took another look at the old town. I wanted to look at it once more and compare it to the time when I was in camps there. I satisfied myself and proceeded on my homeward journey to the old red hills of Georgia, which I had left five years and two months before.

# The Battle of Bayan
# & Other Battles

James Edgar Allen & John J. Reidy

# Note by the Authors

The facts, as related in this little volume, actually occurred on the dates herein mentioned, and anyone doubt-
ing the authenticity of this statement can easily verify it by
communicating with any of the persons mentioned within
these pages, or by consulting the files of any leading News-
paper or Magazine, nearly all of which published accounts
of the affairs shortly after they occurred.

*The Authors*

# The Soldier's Death in Mindanao

*The lone shades of evening have fallen o'er the white tented plain,*
*And the sun has sank deep in the horizon of the watery main.*
*The Camp is all silent, the banners are waving no more,*
*And the sound of the waves are echoing from the far distant shore.*
*The tire-worn soldier, fatigued from the march of the day,*
*Is silently sleeping and dreaming of scenes far away.*
*Of his own Native Land where he spent many jovial hours,*
*Of the sweetheart with whom he has roved by the shady*
*    green bowers.*

*He sees in his dreams the cherished home of his boyhood so dear,*
*And the mother he loved as she sits by the fireside in tears.*
*She is thinking of him who has gone from her side to the war*
*To fight the bold Moros in Mindanao's island afar.*
*She is patiently waiting for the bright day of gladness to come,*
*When with arms outstretched she will welcome the warrior home.*
*But lo, as the darkness grows denser in Mindanao's heights,*
*The loud pealing of cannons is heard in the dark stilly night.*

*The trump'ter's call, echoing loud through the hills and ravines,*
*Has aroused the brave soldier from the joy of his*
*    whimsical dreams.*
*He has joined his brave comrades who have formed in line*
*    for the fray,*

*Then he thinks of his mother, his sweetheart and home far away.*
*The battle commences, loud crashes the bolos and spears*
*And the gleam of the bayonets shine forth like the stars*
     *in the sea.*
*Colonel Baldwin's command is now heard by the brave*
     *and the bold,*
*As onward they charge like lions leaping mad at a fold.*

*They meet in hot conflict, they bleed in the midst of the strife,*
*For their country's freedom, for their glory, their honour and life.*
*The battle is over amid cheers from the victors of war,*
*But alas, one brave hero has fallen with many a scar.*
*Bleeding he lays on the field in his anguish and pain,*
*Whose dreams were of home, of the loved one he will*
     *never see again.*
*He pictures, in anguish, his mother in sorrow and gloom,*
*Vainly waiting for him who will never return to his home.*

*The black cloud of death darkens o'er the young soldier so brave,*
*Then he dies, and with honour is borne to his rest in the grave.*
*But the mother waits on, no news from the young hero comes,*
*For he sleeps with the brave where he fell, in a warrior's tomb.*

John J. Reidy

# Preface

In after years, especially when one has lived to survive a great battle, it is sometimes a pleasant thing to be able to recall to memory the scenes of by-gone days. But this cannot always be done in the desired form without some outside aid. Accordingly, this little volume is published for that very purpose, and the authors earnestly hope that it will meet with the approval of all those who were fortunate enough to survive those memorable events.

It has been the aim of the authors to give an unbiased description of the Battles, just as they occurred, and it is expressly desired that the public as well may derive some satisfaction from a perusal of the following pages.

# The Battle of Bayan

As I sit here on the demolished walls of Fort Pandapatan, contemplating the magnificent scene spread out before me, my mind reverts to that awful Battle fought on the 2nd of May of this year, which was rightfully designated by General Adna R. Chaffee as the hardest fought battle of the entire Philippine insurrection. And as I look down the grassy slopes of Pandapatan hill, and across the open towards Binidayan hill, on which once stood that impregnable Moro stronghold, Fort Binidayan, I can see in fancy those advancing lines of determined men and hear the awful screech of flying projectiles, just as if that terrible drama of reality were being enacted over again for my own especial benefit.

And while I am in the mood and have the inspiration to do so, I shall endeavour to convey to the reader a slight conception of what the Battle was like, and how it appeared to me on that eventful day, and which will go down in history as one of the most glorious feats of American arms.

I can see again, in fancy, that column of determined fighting men, at the head of which rode General (then Colonel) Frank D. Baldwin, struggling over the slippery

mountain trails, fording the swift running rivers, and swel-
tering in the hot tropical sun, just as they did on April 17,
18, and 19, 1902.

It does not seem that several months have elapsed since
General Chaffee issued an ultimatum to the Sultan of Bayan and other leading Moros of the Lake region, demanding
the surrender of several Moro tribesmen for the murder of
Pvts. Lewis and Mooris of the 27th Infantry, in March last,
and for the return of several horses which had been de-
liberately stolen from Lieut. Forsyth, 15th Cavalry, at Bul-
doon, a small village in the mountains along the south coast
of Mindanao.

When General Chaffee visited the little town of Malabang in the early part of April, inviting the Sultans and
Dattos of the Lake region to come in and hold a friendly
conference with him, little did he dream that he was taking
the first step in what was to be one of the most aggressive
campaigns ever inaugurated.

But when, instead of complying with the terms of the
ultimatum, the Moros insolently replied to it and defied
the Americans to come and fight, General Chaffee realized
then that the situation was grave indeed, and accordingly
telegraphed to Washington immediately for permission to
proceed to the Lake region and administer a lesson to the
recalcitrant Sultans and Dattos.

But it was not until after much delay that the War Department reluctantly gave permission to proceed against
the Moros, and General Chaffee was cautioned not to go
to the extreme of warfare, until every peaceful method had
been exhausted

## The First Advance

Preparations were at once begun; an expedition was
formed and got in readiness, and on April 17, 1902, six

companies of the 27th Infantry, two troops of the 15th Cavalry, and the 25th Battery of Field Artillery started for the interior of Mindanao, which had, as yet, never been explored by white men.

The troops constituting that column were, for the most part, raw material, having been organized but a short time previous to the time of which I write, and had as yet seen but little of active service.

But it must not be imagined that they were all inexperienced in warfare, for in its ranks were many who had either transferred from other organizations or who had voluntarily enlisted in these organizations, and who had seen service in more than one war.

It is needless to narrate how the column marched over the first great mountain range which follows along the southern coast in a parallel line, and then on to the enemy infested region about Lake Dapao, which is but a forerunner of a more impregnable region, and which is now gradually resuming its former peaceful aspect, and which in time will develop into one of the most productive regions in the Philippine Archipelago.

## THE ENEMY ENCOUNTERED

Suffice it to say that after three days of hardships and privation, those troops, constituting what was known as the "Lake Lanao Expedition," encountered the enemy on a bit of rising ground at a place known as Gadungan, and after two engagements fought, one there, and one at a place known as Fort Pualos, a camp was established in that vicinity and negotiations with the Moros were renewed.

These were but preliminary engagements and were merely forerunners of what was to come.

After a useless delay and fruitless attempt to restore peace, the column again advanced, this time for the Bayan Forts.

On May 1 the little army of American troops arrived at a point on the south-eastern shore of Lake Lanao, overlooking the Lake and in sight of the enemy's stronghold.

At this juncture Brigadier General George W. Davis, commanding the Seventh Separate Brigade, and who had been designated by General Chaffee to personally accompany the expedition, arrived from Malabang after making a flying trip across the mountains.

A temporary camp was established and General Davis prepared messages in Arabic writing, which were immediately sent to the Sultan of Bayan, demanding his surrender by noon of May 2, or suffer the consequences.

These messages are known to have been delivered but they were not replied to.

### Preliminary Firing

During the night of May 1, the American outposts were fired upon frequently by the Moros, but they did not reply to the fire of the enemy.

At daylight camp was broken, and the column pushed ahead in the direction of Bayan. The column was halted about one half mile from the first fort.

The Moro outposts opened fire on the Americans, but they were not replied to.

The Americans were waiting for twelve o'clock.

About one thousand yards to the right and front was a small clump of bamboo, several natives appeared there, firing a few shots and flourishing their weapons, all the time yelling like mad. It was now plainly seen that the Moros were determined to have war.

The Artillery was brought into play and trained on the clump of bamboo on the right, also Fort Binidayan, which was situated on the crest of a high hill about fifteen hundred yards distant.

Those were indeed moments of suspense for those gallant troops, but not a shot was fired by them, although they were under an almost constant fire from the enemy.

But just at twelve o'clock, General Davis stepped forward, watch in hand, and took one long, lingering look in the direction of Fort Binidayan, and then, not seeing any signs of a peace envoy, but, on the contrary, every indication of hostility, he turned slowly to Captain W. S. McNair, of the 25th Battery, and gave the signal to "let her go."

*Boom*, echoed the little mountain guns, and away went a shrapnel screaming across the open and just three and six-tenths seconds after, exploded immediately over the fort.

Instantly figures were seen hurrying to and fro about the fort. *Boom!* went another, this time at the clump of bamboo on the right.

A puff of smoke, and then,—a cloud of dust immediately in front of the bamboo—told the tale only too well to the gunners.

The battle of the Bayan forts had begun.

Quick movements were observed here and there, companies were being assigned their positions, orders were being transmitted like lightning from point to point, and in less time than it takes to narrate it, that body of men were swung into action like the pendulum of a clock.

The work of demolishing the Binidayan Fort had now begun in earnest, companies "F" and "G" of the 27th Infantry advanced in line of skirmishers, while the Artillery continued a slow fire on the Fort, company "H" joined "F," and crossed the intervening ridge and then through the little valley, while "G" went off to the right, to flank

Binidayan and at the same time to make a demonstration against Fort Pandapatan, which was to the right and rear of Binidayan.

Fort Pandapatan was the second fort known as the system of Bayan forts, of which there are four.

At the base of the Binidayan hill the Infantry halted for an instant, and then started up the hill in a long, thin line of skirmishers, with determination written in their faces.

It was the initial event of the kind for many of them, but every head was erect, every man in his place.

There was not a bit of confusion, simply an orderly line of men coming up to do battle. They were under a constant fire from the enemy while they were advancing but they did not reply to them until they were close enough to plainly distinguish the heads of the Moros bobbing up and down in the trenches which surrounded the Fort.

They laid down prone on the ground then and poured a withering fire into the fort and trenches, which quickly routed the enemy.

## THE CHARGE

Suddenly, back on the ridge where the Artillery were stationed the clear notes of a bugle were heard, sounding "Charge." Instantly those blue shirted figures away up on the grassy slope, rose as if by magic, and then pressed forward and upward, with a yell that was sufficient in itself to route the enemy, and it did route them, for the Moros were fleeing and falling back on Fort Pandapatan by hundreds.

The troops reached the very walls and there paused for an instant—to gain breath, then a command rang out, clear and cool, and it seemed that one mighty wave swept on and over the walls, and in an instant more, those standing back on the ridge where the Artillery was, saw "Old Glory" unfurled to the breeze from the shattered walls of Fort Binidayan.

The first position of the enemy had been taken without loss to the Americans.

But not so fortunate for the Moros, for here and there a mangled body of a dusky warrior dotted nature's carpet, some already dead, others breathing their last, but stubbornly defying the Americans to do their worst. At this stage of the battle there came a distinct lull in the firing, and both sides took advantage of it to "take a hitch" and prepare for the real battle, which was yet to come.

During this lull the Artillery closed up and took their new position on Binidayan hill, a little to the south of the fort.

Floating over Fort Pandapatan there were no less than twenty large red flags.

Most of the Moros had already fallen back on this stronghold and they could plainly be seen, throwing up extra entrenchments.

It was now two o'clock and the real work was about to begin.

Companies "E" and "F" started straight down the Binidayan hill in the direction of Pandapatan, while "B" Company was sent to the right. After the Infantry had crossed the little valley in front, the Artillery opened up and the big fight was on.

## THE REAL BATTLE BEGINS

The shell and shrapnel flew fast and furious from those little mountain guns, accompanied by the music of the "Krags."

On and on, nearer and nearer up the hillside came the crash of advancing troops, smothering other unseen trenches on their way, until by nightfall there was not a rifle but could shove its muzzle into the very face of the trench behind which the Moro warriors laid in waiting, peering down the slope between the explosions for something they feared more than the whistling fragments of Krupp shells—the blue-shirted form of the silent American soldier, with whom the Moros knew the ultimate issue rested.

### Exceptional Courage

On they came, however, up the hill, silent and straight, hundreds of them, right into the open below the trench from behind which the Moros delivered a withering fire and gasped at the folly of the Americans.

Up and up they came, the lower *lantacas* blasting them off the face of the earth, but still they rushed on and upward against the frowning walls.

The mountain guns howled and roared over them, the walls grew troubled and shaky, falling in and falling out, dimly seen between the curtain of smoke and sheet of flame whirling about the leaping stones. But steady eyes were gleaming where they could through the sheets of fire, and steady fingers were pulling triggers rapidly and incessantly.

The crash came unbroken and clearly heard from the midst of the uproar thundering up at the trench, as if the shells were bursting with a million rattling fragments, and down the slope were tumbling the blue-shirted figures, one under that tree, two over there by the big boulder, another here and a dozen more down there, and during the next two hours there was the most magnificent display of true courage and grit ever heard of or seen.

The Artillery roared in anger and anguish, but apparently of no avail, for the long streams of fire continued to pour from the fort with regular intervals, and more blue-shirted figures went tumbling down the hill.

But this did not continue very long, for the Artillery turned loose all its little dogs of war and they barked fiercely and hurled death projectiles into the fort and trenches with renewed vigour.

Think how you would feel if a person should hurl a stone at you with a tremendous shout.

Multiply the stone and shout by twenty millions, add fire and smoke and nauseous vapours, and imagine the earth trembling beneath your feet, with the air filled with screaming projectiles, even then you cannot imagine the terror of that Artillery assault.

### Defiant to the Last

But the fanatical Moros would not give up; there they stood in the very midst of that hurricane of death, calm, immovable, and indifferent to it all. Their resistance could not help but be admired as they stood there calm and defiant, against that advancing, enveloping thunderstorm of musketry. But it must not be imagined that they were idle; far from it. If one can imagine taking a handful of pebbles and hurling them with a strong force against a pane of glass, then, and then only, can one imagine the whirlwind of bullets which the Moros were pouring into that little army of Americans out there in the open.

When it is considered that the Americans were out in the open storming this fort while the Moros were strongly fortified and deeply entrenched, the fierceness of the battle and the heroism of the troops can be imagined. Nothing like it had ever been seen before and nothing like it ever will be seen again. Regardless of bullets and the flying fragments of shell and shrapnel, Baldwin's men kept steadily onward and upward, until they were within a few yards of that impregnable wall, through whose portholes there poured a constant stream of fire. It was like gazing through the doors of a red hot furnace. And all the time the swarm of blue-shirted figures rolled on and upward until they could have dropped a stone over the wall.

They had now gone the limit, as they were very near the

dangerous zone of the exploding shrapnel and were compelled to halt to keep from being struck by their own men.

## The Walls Tremble

Suddenly, back on the hill where the little dogs of war were barking, a command was heard, "Battery, Fire!" and the air was filled with flying projectiles which went screaming and screeching across the open and striking the walls of the fort with a mighty impact, that structure was shaken to its very foundations. Even untouched, one felt shaky and uncertain on that hillside, and one would have felt his body rending to pieces as he looked where a shell burst in the midst of a trench, and heard the filthy squelch and sharp cries above the roar, and saw the awful faces through the red glare and curtain of smoke, and the mangled corpses of dead bodies hurled high in the air. It would make a thrilling scene for some great war drama. The history of war has had few situations as thrilling as this day's battle.

The artillery "let itself go" again and it was impossible to stand on that hillside, so fiercely was the breath of the shells blasting across it in hot, staggering gusts, the tall dry grass bending before it, and the air filled with flying debris, which followed in the wake of a shell in little circling whirlwinds. Skimming but a few feet over the heads of the American fighting line, the shells would burst upon the trenches or on the ground below them, when attackers were so close to attacked that the gush of oily smoke hid both, and both the death yell and the yell of triumph were mingled in one mighty shout and ceaseless roaring.

## The Enemy's Colours Fall

Boom! went the little war dogs, then boom,—boom—boom—boom, in quick succession, and then the wall crumbled, vanished in parts, and lo! behold! the flags were down! Their crimson colours were dangling in mid air for an instant, then were caught in the shower of a bursting shrapnel and hurled to the ground.

Oh! the grandeur of that last few moments' bombardment! Not a shell went astray; the parapet received them all full in the face. In one great explosion the Moros stood and fired, in one atmosphere of blasted air and filthy fumes, in one terrible shadow of the coming darkness, in one continual earthquake. They seemed to go mad, as well they might, for annihilation loomed in the distance for those who yet remained. As the soldiers of America drew nearer, many of the Moros actually leaped from their cover on to the top of the parapet and were seen against the sky background, wildly firing down at the advancing troops, in the very midst of the bursting shells. Hell was surely let loose on those dusky fanatics who manned the portholes of Pandapatan. Truly, war is hell!

They fought with a fanatical frenzy, but nothing on earth could stop that line of advancing, invincible soldiers. Up they went, until at last, it became necessary for the artillery to cease firing.

The troops reached the very walls, and there remained, for entrance was impossible.

However, after fighting hand to hand until dark, the outer trenches were taken. With the capture of these trenches the enemy's position was practically won. But the Moros did not yet give up; on the contrary they made preparations to resist to the death. They had sworn to die in battle, and they were admirably carrying out the oath.

### SUFFERINGS OF THE WOUNDED

Darkness had fallen now and it began to rain in torrents. Night fell terribly for the wounded out there. That awful cry, "Doctor! This way. Help!" can be heard to this day. It continued throughout the night, but not in vain, for the artillerymen were out there all night carrying the wounded off the field and rendering valuable aid to the surgeons. These men worked like heroes every one, and deserve the greatest credit for the magnificent gallantry shown during that terrible night's work while under a constant fire from the enemy.

## THE DEFIANT SULTAN'S DOWNFALL

It seemed that a difficult problem lay before the Americans that night. It was proposed that a number of scaling ladders be made and that the place be carried by assault. Accordingly, construction on these ladders was begun at once, but they were destined never to be used, for at daylight the white flags were fluttering over the fort and Pandapatan had fallen.

## A GRUESOME SIGHT

At last the big fight was over. After nearly twenty-four hours of continual firing the Americans had conquered. It had been a splendid battle, and what manner of death the vanquished had suffered only those who looked into the fort and trenches after the battle, can say. The mangled bodies of the Moro dead were piled up eight and ten deep in places, and only those acquainted with the technicalities of a slaughter house can imagine the sight as it appeared the next morning after the battle. But these people would have war, and war they got, in all its glory. Just eighty-three survivors remained out of the hundreds that resisted the Americans.

But it must not be imagined that this great victory had been achieved without loss to the Americans. Their casualties were far greater than those of an ordinary battle, numbering close to a hundred.

With the break of day the gruesome task of burying the dead began, and continued throughout the day, and by nightfall of May 3rd the Battle of Bayan was over and passed, but I cannot say forgotten, for that can never be, for the memory of that battle will ever dwell in the minds of those who witnessed or participated in that never-to-be-forgotten event.

*James Edgar Allen*

# Rewards

To receive praise for work accomplished, no matter in what form, is certainly pleasing to every phase of humanity. And to be rewarded for our work gives us a certain feeling of satisfaction, and assures us that our work along a certain line has been appreciated and admired. But to a soldier, whose duty is to do battle, praise for his victories is more than pleasing—it is exalting. And when after struggling along almost indefinitely at a certain task, and finally accomplishing it with overwhelming success, he is commended by anxious relatives and friends, usually the height of his ambition has been reached.

But to be especially commended and congratulated for his achievements, and by his superior officers and his commander-in-chief especially, is one of the highest honours that could be conferred upon him.

When he has performed deeds of true valour and courage, wherein he exhibits exceptional bravery, and is almost overwhelmingly besieged with letters of congratulation and praise, he has received one of the greatest of earthly rewards. But there are other rewards, such as promotion, for instance, and one has but to consult our army records at Washington to find that many of those who constituted what is known as the Lake Lanao Expedition have been fittingly rewarded for their gallant services on the 2nd day of May, 1902. That the reader may judge of the magnificent gallantry shown by those troops on that eventful day, a few of the letters are hereby published in full.

COPY OF CONGRATULATORY MESSAGES

Camp Vicars (Mind.), P. I.
May 7, 1902
Announcement
The troops of the Lake Lanao Expedition have been paraded in order that the following messages may be read to them:

First
Manila
May 4, 1902
To General Davis
Order that the following message of the President of the United States be read to every company and troop in your Brigade. It will be published in Division Orders for the information of other commanders, and as a special mark and tribute to the assaulting force of the Battle of Bayan.
(Sgd.) *Chaffee*

President's Message
Washington, D. C.
May 5, 1902
To General Chaffee
Manila
Accept for the Army under your command, and express to General Davis and Colonel Baldwin especially, my congratulations and thanks for the splendid

courage and fidelity which has again carried our flag to victory. Your fellow countrymen at home will ever reverence the memory of the fallen, and be faithful to the survivors, who have themselves been faithful unto death for their country's sake.

*Theodore Roosevelt*

Second
Manila,
May 4, 1902
To General Davis
Please accept my congratulations for yourself, and express to Colonel Baldwin and all the officers and men engaged in the Battle of May 2, my high appreciation of their bravery, gallantry and soldiery conduct. My congratulations to both officers and men. I sincerely regret the death of some and the wounding of others. Let no comfort be withheld from the latter that can be supplied them.

*A. R. Chaffee*
General
Commanding Philippines

Third
Cebu
May 4, 1902
To General Davis
My sincere congratulations to Baldwin, and to the officers and men engaged yesterday. Also to yourself for your energetic and skilful conduct of the whole affair, from first to last. It was necessary to give the Moros a lesson, and it seems to have been done in such a manner that it will not have to be repeated.

*Wade*
Brigadier General

Fourth

Remarks of General George W. Davis

*Soldiers*

Words at my command fail to convey an adequate expression of admiration for the gallantry and self-sacrifice which I saw displayed by the assaulting lines and investing cordon on the 2nd of May. The memory of this sanguinary action will be treasured by all participants and observers as long as they live. For the 27th Infantry and the 25th Battery of Field Artillery, Bayan will always be an inspiration. At this moment of exaltation and triumph do not forget the vanquished foe, whose persistent gallantry commanded the admiration of all who saw the magnificent defence of their stronghold. A race of men who have been able to make such a fight, and who have turned this wilderness into a garden, have many qualities which if guided right will make them and their posterity valuable citizens. None can doubt who have seen what they have accomplished without the aid which civilized people enjoy. Let no word or act be brought home to the American soldier that discredits or disparages these Moros. Let it be the unremitting effort of every officer and soldier to assist and elevate them, a sacred duty which is devolved upon the Army, an added burden which must be borne; and every American relies upon our troops to execute this sacred trust. So far there has been no act of wanton despoilment, injury or insult; let none ever be charged to an American soldier. Our flag is an emblem of freedom and honour, and it remains with you that it shall become such an emblem to the Moros, and ever so remain.

*George W. Davis*

Brigadier General, U. S. A.

Commanding Seventh Separate Brigade

Fifth
Headquarters
Lake Lanao Expedition
Camp Vicars (Mind.), P. I.
May 7, 1902
Announcement
The commanding officer appreciates the gallantry of
his regiment. The encounter of the 19th, 20th, and
21st of April, ending in the capture of Fort Pualos,
and on May 2nd in the capture of nine fortified positions and the final overcoming of a most desperate
enemy, in a thoroughly equipped fortification known
as Fort Pandapatan, where our losses were far greater
than those of an ordinary battle, is the initial event in
the history of the Regiment, and has set a high standard of valour and courage which will never be low-
ered as long as the 27th Infantry exists. He also desires
to express his high appreciation of the gallantry and
devotion to duty of the 25th Battery of Field Artillery,
and desires that they consider the foregoing remarks
concerning his regiment apply equally to them.
*F. D. Baldwin*
Colonel
Commanding 27th Infantry

## Sermon on Courage

Following is a copy of the admirable sermon preached
by Chaplain George D. Rice of the 27th Infantry, to the
troops of the Lake Lanao Expedition, on the Sunday following the battle of Bayan:"I am going to speak to you
to-day on courage, and how I saw it displayed on May 2nd,
while you were engaged in open combat with the Moros.

There was a time when I thought that true courage
was the absence of fear. But after witnessing the battle

of this week I have seen that which has caused me to think differently now, because you demonstrated to me on that day that true courage is not the absence of fear, but the conquest of it. Surely, yours was the highest order of courage.

I recollect when 'E' Company came to re-enforce. I turned and watched three men in skirmish line coming through the tall grass under heavy fire from the fort. They knew they were coming into the thickest of the fire, but the interval in that line was correct, every piece right, no shouting or noise of any sort. Simply a perfect line of determined men coming up to take part.

'Tis more than courage, I thought. It is order, it is discipline and coolness. And the wounded! Such courage! One man struck in the leg. We would help him to the rear; but no, he could crawl and refused help. Another hit in the right arm, and he laughed. Then a bullet struck his left arm and he only smiled and said: 'They did not treat me like this in the Panay campaign.'

Lieut. Wagner was shot in the stomach and leg, and said to me: 'My only regret is to leave the fort with my work unfinished.' I saw one soldier whom I supposed was dead, I pulled a shelter-half over him; just then a soldier came running by. An officer shouted, 'Where are you going?' 'My ammunition is all gone,' replied the man. I saw the shelter-half move. In a moment my supposed dead man was sitting upright. He removed his belt containing a few cartridges and gave it to the soldier. I wish I could remember this man, but there were twenty or thirty dead and wounded near there, and they were doing brave and unexpected things like this all the time.

Brave Vicars fell, mortally wounded, leading 'F' Company. Lieut. Jossman had hardly time to assume command when he, too, was shot, leaving 'F' Company without an officer, yet his finely disciplined company held its line perfectly. A bullet struck Captain Moore in the head, and as he rolled into one of the ditches he was heard to say, 'Do not retreat.' I saw a wounded soldier making a noble effort to get out of the line of fire. Who would help him? 'I'm going to help that man if I die for it,' I heard someone say, as the man repeatedly tottered and fell, with a terrible wound in his side. I looked, and in a moment brave Lieut. Bickham, tall and strong, was facing the numerous shot and shell to save his man, and he succeeded. A bullet passed through Major Scott's hat, grazed his head, and brought the Major to his knees, but this officer remained on the line.

During that awful fight I saw officers and men leave their positions in front of those terrible portholes for two reasons only—either because wounded or to get more ammunition.

There were hundreds of instances of heroism occurring about that fort. When Lieut. Fulmer called for volunteers to scale the walls, dozens of men responded. Lieuts. Hawkins and Wilson performed noble service, and were a credit to themselves and their regiment. Battalion Adjutant Drum, with his face smeared with powder and the dust of battle, was as cool as he was courageous. Captains Phillips, Rogers, Lyons and Hutton were with their respective commands, encouraging their men and doing excellent service.

It was surely a high order of courage that caused Sgt. Graves to swing himself over the outer stockade of Binidayan when the fanatic Moro and his knife could be seen above. It was courage of the most godly type that took Corporal McGoveren down into the trenches to prop up the heads of wounded men and give them water, while fighting, biting, dying Moros occupied the same trenches. It was kingly courage on the part of Corpl. Keeler, who, when shot in the leg, refused help, and said to me, 'I can get to the rear alone, sir; help someone else.' It was courage of the Christian soldier that inspired Sergt. Major Ingold and Sergt. McCarthy, both wounded, to speak words of hope to their comrades.

The courage displayed by the Moros was very different. The Moros were caught in a trap. They knew it, and they fought the desperate fight of their lives. You can drive a mouse into a corner like this, and he, too, will turn. Bravery through necessity is not the true courage which comes of Christ.

Officers and soldiers of the 27th Infantry, I congratulate you to-day. You have been tested and shown what you can do. You deserve credit for what you did, and it is my earnest desire that the credit be equally divided. When you write home to your people and tell them of the gallant victory of the 27th Regiment, I want you to remember to speak of others whose presence and deeds rendered it possible for you to accomplish what you did. I want you to remember the officers and enlisted men of the 25th Battery. After the work of the battery was done, the members of the battery came to the front with litters made of rifles, bamboo poles, ponchos, and shelter-halves, with which they picked up many wounded and took them to the surgeon. These men came to the line in squads, each with litters, asking for wounded men, and several wounded men owe their lives to these brave batterymen. They would go anywhere to get a wounded man. They faced the thickest of the fire. A wounded man was pointed out in a bunch of grass, and the bullets struck there so fast that one could see the grass cut off. But these Artillerymen went there, and in a few moments had the man safe in a litter. And all night these noble fellows kept up the work. They took wounded from the jungles, the trenches and the open, and carried them to a place of safety. Let us never forget the work of the officers and men of the 25th Battery.

Captain McNair, and Lieutenants Clark, Sunderland, and Deems of this battery are worthy of our praise and thanks. Major Porter, surgeon, tried to get on the line to treat a wounded man when a shot struck him and brave Porter had to be taken to the rear. Just behind him I saw hospital corps man Johnson also trying to reach a wounded man when Johnson fell into one of the terrible and dark pitfalls of the enemy, but got out later and did good work with the wounded. Young Dr. Allan deserves credit for dressing numberless wounds of officers and men in the trenches close to the fort and under fire that day. Drs. LeCompte and Grabenstatter worked like heroes. Major Anderson, chief surgeon of the expedition, made every preparation possible for the care of the wounded officers and enlisted men. The entire medical corps remained up all night attending to the wounded. They deserve great credit for their work on that rainy, chilly and dark night under the fire of the enemy.

And do not forget the men of the pack-train. Do you know that these men brought a pack-train of ammunition to you over the slippery dangerous trail that night?

Captains Shuttleworth and Andrus, Lieutenants Peck and Fries and their packers worked hard for you. They toiled constantly until they had every wounded officer and man supplied with tentage, cots, blankets, and clean clothes. Likewise, kindly remember the engineers and signal corps men. Their work in this expedition will never be forgotten. Our commanding officer, Colonel Baldwin, never rested that night. He was up and planning for the morrow and for you. General Davis and his orderly and a small guard rode many miles that night to the next camp below to arrange for more troops to come up.

Thus spoke Chaplain Rice, equally dividing the credit of the victory, and praising all for their part taken in the battle. But in all his words there is one thing that he failed to do, which is characteristic of this noble man. He failed to mention his own gallant services, of which too much praise cannot be given. Almost from the beginning of hostilities he was on the firing line, and up near the fort, speaking words of cheer and comfort to the men in the trenches, and "God bless the chaplain," are the words of every man of the Lake Lanao Expedition.

James Edgar Allen.

# Battle of Gauan

It is night again, the battle of Bayan is now fought and indeed very gloriously won. The last reports of the yet warm cannon have ceased to echo through the distant hills and ravines. The khaki-clad warriors and laurel-crowned victors, blood stained and weary from the struggle of the recent battle, have sought a well earned and much needed repose. But their sleep is not one of comfort or rest, for they have contentedly lain down uncovered on the cold damp ground.

The shrill notes of the bugle call them from their dreamy slumbers at an early hour and their first duty is to finish burying the dead and lend what aid is possible to the sick and wounded, who were too sick and exhausted at this time to be removed over the rugged trails to the hospitals at Malabang.

To do this it was absolutely necessary to establish a camp, somewhere adjacent to the centre of hostilities.

It was then that the post of Camp Vicars, now so widely known throughout the nations of the earth, first had its origin. It was so named in honour of the brave and ever dauntless soldier, Lieut. Vicars, who unfortunately lost his life from a wound received, while heroically engaged in the capture of the stronghold.

Everything is now placid, hostilities had ceased for a time at least, the Moros driven as they were from their forts, and stockades, which had been their sole protection for centuries past against all foreign invasion, had sought shelter from the yet unconquered tribes wherever it could be had, offering scarcely any resistance or hostilities to the troops then at the camp.

## General Chaffee Arrives

General Adna R. Chaffee soon afterwards paid a visit to the recently established camp, arriving with his escort May 10, 1902.

He was given a full account of the battles hitherto fought in that region—Bayan included—from officers who themselves had been daring participants in all the fights.

He immediately decided to send messages to the principal sultans and dattos, who were then commanding tribes of savage *bolomen* along the most impassable regions of the lake shores. The subject matter of his messages were authoritative invitations to come into the camp and hold a friendly conference with him.

He received favourable replies from many of them and two days later the following named sultans and dattos decided to respond to his invitation: Sultan of Genassi; Sultan Amai Tampugao of Tubaran; Sultan of Binidayan; Datto Sa Bayang of Bayan; Datto Pedro of Uato; Datto Agar of Makadah; Datto Agato of Madatlum; Datto Amay Mala-Mala of Taburan; Datto Amay Magatano of Binidayan.

After they had reported it was thought that the greater part of the Moro trouble had subsided. But this was not so—far from it. Their terms of peace were, to say the least, short lived, for in the early part of the month of July a detachment of men was brutally and unexpectedly attacked by a band of *bolomen* on the trail. They were outnumbered by the enemy, and consequently many of the Americans were wounded and some three or four killed outright.

## Treaties Broken

It was now very evident, judging from their recreant action, that the natives had broken all treaties of peace and violated the laws of friendship, so honourably laid down by the Americans.

This evidence of their recriminating and rebellious nature was doubly substantiated, when on August 1st the Sultan of Bacolod, who until then had remained peaceable, sent to Captain J. J. Pershing, commander of the troops at Camp Vicars, the following insolent message, which is translated below for the benefit of our readers:

> We ask you to return to the sea because you should not be here among civilized Moros, for you are not religious. If you stay here we will fight you this month, and in no event will be your friends, because you eat pork. We say to you that if you do not leave this region, come here and the Sultan will sacrifice you, and if you do not wish to come we will come to you and fight.

This was followed in a few days by another message to the commanding officer, from the Sultan of Maciu, which was also of a defiant nature.

Circumstances now began to look rather grave at Camp Vicars. The Americans had endeavoured by every means in their power to prevent further hostilities and trouble, but had failed in all their efforts to bring about peace between themselves and the dark-skinned natives of the trackless plains of Mindanao.

## A Bloody Deed

The Moros did not, however, make any advances until

the night of August 12, when the most appalling and most ghastly murder that has ever been witnessed took place about two hundred yards from the camp. The moon had disappeared temporarily behind a dark cloud, the men had all retired for the night, and everything seemed tranquil, when suddenly the camp was aroused by the firing of shots in rapid succession by the members of the outpost.

The trumpeter was now calling every slumberer to arms, and in a few moments the entire garrison was ready for action. The cries of the men for help and the crashing of the bolos and spears could be heard in the calmness of the dark stilly night. There was no time for idle thoughts, no time to be wasted, for it was evident from their appealing cries that the members of outpost No. 4 had been attacked by the blood-thirsty Moros. Lieut. Bickham, commanding Company "F," proceeded in all haste to cross the deep ravine and reinforce the brave men, who, though outnumbered by a large majority, were nevertheless fighting desperately for their lives.

They arrived on the scene too late to prevent the massacre and death of their fallen comrades, for the savages had by this time made well their escape, after performing one of the most savage, most treacherous and most blood-curdling deeds, that has ever hitherto been recorded in the pages of bloody history.

Not content with killing their victims, they had cut them with their *bolos* and long spears, until their bodies were beyond recognition. The killed were Sergeant Foley and Pvt. Carey of Co. "G," 27th U. S. Infantry, men whose gallantry, kindness, bravery, and social disposition had won for them the admiration of not only the members of their own company, but of everybody who knew them.

The wounded were Pvts. VanDorn and Christianson, also of Co. "G."

Perhaps never in the history of battles and wars did men fight with such grim determination and fearlessness in the very face of death, as did VanDorn and Christianson of Co. "G." Having fallen to the ground from loss of blood and exhaustion, they still bravely clung with untiring tenacity to their rifles and never once flinched or even thought of retreating to a place of safety until the reinforcements had arrived on the bloody scene and the natives had vanished in the underbrush. An investigation ensued which disclosed the fact that the attacking parties belonged to the tribes of Datto Amay Grar.

Immediately afterwards what was to be the last ultimatum was issued to the Moros of the Lake region, particularly to the Sultan of Bacolod and the Sultan of Maciu demanding, rigidly, an explanation regarding the recent attacks upon the Americans, as well as the immediate surrender of the murderers in their tribes who were guilty of committing various acts of injustice and cruelty since the historical battle of May 2.

Their replies were, as usual, of a defiant, insolent, and sullen nature.

The Americans, seeing that the restoration of peace in the island of Mindanao could not be brought about by fair and honourable means, decided to administer a lesson to them that they would not very readily forget.

### Hostilities Renewed

An expedition was organized on short notice, commanded by Capt. J. J. Pershing, of the 15th Regiment of Cavalry, a man whose never failing courage, valour, and ability as an officer and commander is unexcelled in the American Army.

Every preparation was made for the coming events, and

on September 17, at midnight, what was known as Captain Pershing's expedition left Camp Vicars under cover of darkness and proceeded through rugged trails to Maciu's strongholds and neighbouring principalities.

The expedition consisted of Companies "F," "G," "C," and "M" of the 27th Infantry; Troop "L" 15th Regiment of Cavalry; and the 25th Battery of Field Artillery.

On the morning of the 18th, as the first refulgent beams of "Old Sol" had begun to illuminate the eastern horizon, the column had reached and halted close by Fort Gauan, and ere another hour had elapsed the entire fortification was surrounded by our troops.

The 25th Battery had halted directly in front of, and about 300 yards from, the fort, while companies "M" and "F," "G" and "C" had formed skirmish lines on the left and right of the fort. The command was given for the first shot to be fired and everybody waited in silent expectancy for the outcome. In an instant there was a flash, and "bang" went the projectile with lightning velocity, hitting the outer breastworks of the enclosure, from which rose vast clouds of smoke and fragments.

The firing from the fort was rapid at first, but gradually diminished as the outer bombardment continued, and finally ceased altogether, for the Artillery onslaught had been terrible while it lasted, and nothing remained of that once impregnable fortress save a few shattered walls, with here and there the mangled corpse of a dead Moro.

The day was gradually drawing to a close, which made it necessary for us to establish a temporary camp for the night.

This was done, and very fortunately, adjacent to a small river, which proved to be a great convenience to both men and animals.

Natives fired frequently into the midst of the camp, but fortunately without any serious casualty to the Americans.

The first faint glimmer of dawn that broke over the eastern hill-tops found us again in readiness and, after partaking of a hurried breakfast, we broke camp and again took up the trail, this time in the direction of Bayubao.

## Bayubao Vanquished

The trails were, in a great many places, almost impassable, making marching with equipments very laborious. However, we arrived at Bayubao about 2 p.m. and rested for refreshments on the top of a high hill, which over-looked the fort and the unruffled waters of Lake Lanao.

We had not been long in the enjoyment of our much needed rest, when the natives, who were until then concealed in the brush, poured a volley into our midst. The entire column was immediately summoned to action, and a grander sight could not be witnessed than to see that body of brave and disciplined soldiers taking their respective places and falling into line for action.

The Battery was brought into action on the hill-top, with the guns carefully trained on the fort by reliable and experienced marksmen, then a noise arose which seemed to echo back from the very firmaments as if the giant and mighty mountains had left their very sockets and were tumbling in a confused mass into the deep waters of the lake below.

The Battery had cut loose and "let her go," and projectile after projectile was sent from the guns on the hill-top "straight home" and into the very midst of the fort, enveloping everything for a moment in clouds of smoke and flying fragments, which was almost suffocating.

Oh! what a strange feeling influences the soldier when he hears the first "Boom" of a cannon, for full well he knows that it is only a stepping stone leading to the midst of the fray.

The natives returned the fire slowly but steadily, and in a manner that was creditable, for they were not only taken by surprise but were at a critical disadvantage owing to the elevation. Still the firing kept up and more than one dark-skinned foeman could be seen falling, rifle in hand, lifeless on the green sward.

They were now growing confused, ungovernable, and were firing recklessly like savage maniacs at the unflinching column of brave American soldiers, who were coolly aiming and firing at the commands of the valiant officers whenever a well directed shot was to be had. It now appeared evident that before this rain of bullets from the Infantry and the bursting of shrapnel from the Artillery they could not withstand much longer, and our position was such that to hit us at such a range and elevation was almost impossible.

Again the Battery opened up with one last and mighty sheet of solid shot and shrapnel, which made the very walls tremble and shake like the leaves of a forest before a hurricane, and then deathlike shrieks could be heard from within, the stout walls had crumbled to a thousand atoms, and the Sultan of Bayubao, with many of his tribesmen, had fallen to rise no more.

### In Sight of Maciu

But was this to be our last battle with the Moros? Was this to be our last fight in the desolate island of Mindanao? No! No! far from it. There yet remained another, and the stumbling block of them all, who was at this time bidding defiance to all invaders, in his fort across the lake, where we could see, from our present position, the red flags of battle waving before the gentle zephyrs of the orient.

This was the Sultan of Maciu, Maciu the warlike, who had hitherto held his stronghold and expansive territories with creditable success for centuries against even the haughty Spanish soldiers. But his day of gloom was fast approaching, when he and his clan of *bolomen* would be compelled to submit to the sons of America, as will be seen by the ensuing pages.

Soon after Fort Bayubao had been taken the column pressed onwards, down the rugged slope of the trail, leading into the fort, and here, being dust-stained, weary, and footsore, we were glad to encamp for the night. But only a few of us slept, for the Moros delivered a steady fire on us from the surrounding brush through the night.

The welcomed morning broke bright and clear over the waters of Lake Lanao, and the soldiers of "Columbia" awoke from a dreamy and restless slumber at the first notes of the bugle. Preparations for the attack on the Sultan of Maciu were immediately begun, but with little or no success, as the trail leading through the thickly wooded flats was blocked in such a way that it was an impossibility for even the Infantry to force their way through.

The Moros, having seen the column advancing on them, set to work to block the trail leading from Bayubao to the Maciu fortress, thinking that the Americans might on reaching this now impassable entrance, decide to return again to Camp Vicars after failing to reach the much talked of stronghold.

### Food Supply Exhausted

Seeing that all else had failed, the Americans began to construct rude rafts with which to cross an arm of the lake which separated them from the Maciu territories. They succeeded in building one in which a detachment of Companies "C" and "M" attempted to cross under a continued fire from the Moros, who were entrenched on the opposite side.

They kept on, however, seemingly regardless of the rain

of bullets until, after a sharp and lively encounter with the enemy, they found it would be impossible to make a landing, so decided to return, but not before they had succeeded in driving the Moros back.

This was the 22nd day of September, we were now five days on the trail in pursuit of the Moros, but had not as yet begun to show any signs of exhaustion from the march or exposure.

It was now evident that our supply of provisions could not last much longer, and in consideration of the fact that the trail, now blocked by the Moros, should be re-opened before we could reach Maciu, it was deemed advisable by Captain Pershing to return to Camp Vicars, in order to rest the troops and to procure more rations.

Consequently on the morning of the 23rd, the column began the long march from the Maciu and Sauir territory to the Camp, arriving in good military order at 7 p.m. same date, with no loss to the Americans. Lines on the Death of Sergeant Foley and Private Carey, Company G, 27th Infantry.

*Here, cold in their graves, near the spot where they fell,*
*In the darkness of night's dismal gloom,*
*Rest two soldiers whose valour could not be excelled,*
*Slumbering in their desolate tombs.*
*Far away from their kindred they are sleeping to-day*
*In Mindanao's untrodden plains,*
*Where their comrades have laid them to moulder away*
*Into dust, in their cold silent graves.*
*By Camp Vicars they fought at the dead hour of night*
*Outnumbered by the savages wild;*
*Until they fell, overpowered, on the sward at the feet*
*Of their foemen, where like soldiers they died.*
*Perhaps far away in their own native land,*
*In the homes of their childhood so dear,*

*Are their mothers awaiting to grasp their kind hands—*
*But alas! they shall wait many years.*
*For their loved ones will never return again*
*To greet them through life's pleasant way,*
*For they are laying in the grass-covered graves where they fell,*
*And are sleeping long ages away.*
*But though death has overtaken those heroes so brave*
*Who fell for their Country's fame,*
*Yet their memory shall always live on the breasts*
*Of their comrades, whom they perished to save.*

John J. Reidy

# The Battle of Maciu

The troops were given five days in which to rest and recuperate, for the reader can easily imagine the hardships, privations, and sufferings which are undergone by soldiers while on the march, especially where there are no roads of any description, save the narrow, rugged, and, in many places, impassable trails, which are met with all through the island of Mindanao.

Therefore it was practically necessary that, after six days of continual marching through the thick brush of this island, they should be given ample time in which to attain that standard of physique which is the most characteristic mark of the American soldier.

It was the morning of the 28th of September, the bright sun had risen gorgeously over the white tented plain, the azure blue sky was now clear, save a few clouds that still rested lazily on the hill-tops, and all nature's splendours and attractions were everywhere to be seen.

To the inexperienced observer it would seem that the Moros and Americans were living together in happy unison with each other in this, the most remote of American garrisons. But this was not so, for ere another hour had dragged itself lazily into the dim, misty past, the sons of fair Columbia were in complete readiness to march from the camp over many a weary mile to measure the cold steel with the defiant, haughty, and semi-savage Sultan of Maciu, and proud to state, under command of Captain John J. Pershing, to whom is justly attributed the success, the achievements, and all conquering abilities of the brave soldiers under his command at Camp Vicars.

### THE EXPEDITION STARTS

The expedition is complete and after being inspected by the Commanding General is not only complimented by him on their general uniformity and appearances, but are also pronounced fit to compete with the most sanguineous and daring adversary.

At 8 a.m. the command "Forward March" was heard by every anxious soldier who was to be a participant in the coming event, and amid the cheers, farewells, and good wishes of our comrades, we advanced in single file from the camp over the now well known trail leading to the territories of the Sultan of Maciu.

The expedition was composed of the same troops as that of the preceding campaign, except in addition there was Troop "A," 15th Cavalry.

The men were by this time beginning to grow accustomed to this singular style of marching from previous experiences, and that, together with the impatient anxiety they had to meet Maciu's tribe in battle, added new strength and vigour to every man as onward they pressed over high hills, through deep ravines and swift-flowing rivers until, with the fire of military and true national determination written on every face, the column arrived and halted once again on the hill-top overlooking the now fallen stronghold of Bayubao with which the reader is already familiar.

No time was lost until we were again encamped at the foot of the hill about 100 yards from the lake shore. We immediately set to work to cook our much needed supper, which was devoured greedily by every dust-stained warrior of the command, regardless of the rules of etiquette, after which we sought a "soft spot" on nature's expansive bed, in which to lay our weary bones for the night.

But even a soldier's life has, despite its many seemingly insurmountable obstacles, many a romantic charm, for who would not like to lay gently upon the lap of earth with the soft side of a haversack for a pillow, and the green foliage of the graceful bamboo trees for a canopy, and be lulled to sleep by the wild rustling of the leaves wafted to and fro before the gentle zephyrs. Everything remained at a peaceable standard during the night with nothing to break the "chain of silence," save the rippling of the waters in the lake below.

But even a sleep such as this, under such unusual and un-accommodating circumstances, has an unwelcomed limit, and ours came with the first streaks of grey dawn that broke through our foliaged canopied beds, and again each soldier of American loyalty began to kindle his fire, with which to cook his breakfast, for on such occasions as this each soldier is his own cook, waiter, and dishwasher combined.

Soon after breakfast the real work of opening the trail began, rifles were quickly supplanted by shovels, picks and axes, and in a very few moments every soldier was equipped with tools, which they began to use with unanimous energy and willingness during the greater part of the day. And it was truly wonderful to see those brave soldiers working untiringly, chopping heavy trees, digging and filling deep ravines, levelling stout barricades, all working diligently for that one aim which was to be the downfall of Maciu.

This work was kept up unceasingly until the passage or trail was opened to the Maciu peninsula, a distance of two miles. It was the afternoon of the second day, which was the 30th of September, before we finally reached our destination, where there was an unexpected surprise in store for us.

## Fired Upon

The natives, having known that our object was to cross through this skirt of woodland, had awaited our arrival on the opposite side. And as soon as the first file of the "advance guard" passed from the woods into the open plain beyond, they met with a storm of bullets from the enemy. They then moved forward into the open beyond as quickly as possible, after which they unanimously returned the enemy's fire. The firing was fast, and not without effect, for ere the gloom of night began to descend upon us, many a native of Mindanao had sacrificed his semi-barbarous life for his freedom.

It now began to grow dark, and fearing lest we should be overtaken by the shadows of night in the dense woods, Captain Pershing gave orders to the column to return to Bayubao for the night.

The trail, our most important obstruction, was now cleared and it was with impatience and sleepless expectancy we awaited the first glimmer of dawn. At last came the day when the true, fearless soldiers were to march against Maciu's tribe. We shared together a hurried breakfast and about 7 a.m. we advanced under the cool shadows of the interwoven foliage, over many a rough boulder, until after two hours of rough marching we arrived in the open space beyond the woods.

We had not marched over three-hundred yards of this new territory when the natives began firing at the head of the column, but without effect, for as soon as the smoke from their rifles could be seen, a volley was fired at them by the soldiers. In a few moments we had gained the summit of the hill, and here we halted to await the arrival of the Battery, which was some distance in the rear, for not more than 400 yards in front of the skirmish line was a fort from which shots were fired at regular and frequent intervals. We did not return the fire this time, knowing as we did that rifle fire was of no avail against a fortification such as this proved itself to be.

The Battery soon arrived, and, in less time than it takes to relate it, they were ready for action, being about 400 yards from the fort. As soon as the first shot from the Artillery was fired the Moros began to abandon the fort and were going in the direction of Maciu. The Infantry had formed a semi-circular skirmish line around the stronghold and now, the Battery having ceased firing, they began to move forward, closing around the fort. At last they reached it and after scaling its high walls, they found that the greater part of its inmates had fled, taking their arms with them. The soldiers soon began to destroy the fort, and in a very few moments it was reduced to ashes.

The column again took up the trail leading towards the lake front destroying, as they went, everything in the shape of forts or strongholds which they encountered, and from which they had been fired upon.

Perhaps the reader may think or imagine our dealings with the Moros of the Lake region to be of a cruel nature. To this I can only state that having been amongst them since the origin of hostilities in the island of Mindanao, up to the present date, and having become rather familiar with their treachery and cruelties to American soldiers, wherever they could get a chance, I think as far as my judgment is concerned that they have been given a lesson which, to say the least, they richly deserve.

We captured some five or six minor fortifications during this day, and towards evening we proceeded towards the lake front, to encamp for the ensuing night, for it was an absolute necessity to procure water for the men and horses, as quickly as possible.

That night was spent in thought, and in anticipation of the doings of the approaching day, for it was the day designated for the capture of the Maciu stronghold. We broke camp at an early hour and at 7 a.m. we were again on the march, this time in a new direction. We had not been marching over two hours when the word was quietly passed along the line that the Maciu stronghold was in sight.

We now began to think more seriously as we were nearing our long looked for destination, for well we knew that the Moros, having consolidated here were determined to fight to the last.

We were, however, perfectly willing and ready to face Maciu and his tribesmen in open combat, and meet whatever fate awaited us, without a murmur.

The column was ordered to deploy right and left in skirmish line, and advance towards the fort, in order that they could more easily and readily command a view of the outer surroundings of the enclosure, and prevent, if possible, the escape of any of the blood-thirsty Moros whose wild cries we could now hear within.

The Battery, having halted in front of the fort, was immediately brought into action. Then suddenly a deafening noise was heard by all, the noise which, though too familiar to many of us, was nevertheless to make even a brave soldier tremble. The Artillery had opened up on the left. "Boom! Boom!!" went the cannons, and a rain of solid shot and shrapnel was hurled at the fort, and for a space of a moment nothing could be seen but the flying fragments, and splinters of bamboo and debris hurled high in the air.

The clouds of smoke soon cleared away and then something happened unexpectedly, and which surprised every

American soldier in that vicinity. A thick, black volume of smoke arose in the direction of the fortress, then a flash, and a deafening noise, as if the merciless waves of the Pacific were beating against the granite ribbed cliffs.

They had replied to our firing. Boom! went the *lantacas*, followed by a volley from the rifles, and then it behoved every true American to "lay low" for a few moments.

It now looked as if our expectations were going to be fulfilled to the last. There was a moment of silence and again the Battery opened up in real earnest, and a more exciting scene could not be witnessed than to see the havoc wrought on that fort by the guns. Bang! Bang!! went the shots in rapid succession, and bamboo, rocks, and flying fragments were hurled hundreds of feet in every direction, but still the Moros kept firing and crying in wild religious ecstasy to their Mohammedan God.

Captain Pershing, who had been coolly riding about the fort to Artillery, Infantry, and Cavalry, now decided to order two of the guns brought to the right of the fort. This was done immediately and from right and left they cut loose, determined to accomplish their aim.

But instead of this, they were surprised, when the Moros poured a withering fire at them and crude lead balls and fragments of iron were dropping in the midst of the troops.

It was now 2 p.m. and it looked as if Maciu's stronghold was impregnable indeed, for we had been firing steadily since 9 a.m. and nothing of importance had, as yet, been accomplished.

The Battery now moved towards the fort from both sides, until they were within fifty yards of them, and it may be well to mention that it never has been known in the history of battles where Artillery has engaged an enemy at so short a range. They had now taken up their new positions and began to fire at the fort from both sides, this time with great effect. But still the Moros remained obstinate to the last singing wildly their religious songs to their God "Allah" in the very midst of the struggle.

The day was now drawing to a close and yet the firing kept on. However, at 4 p.m. the command "cease firing" was given, and with that ended that day's struggle for us, but not for the natives, for they, thinking that the Americans were about to abandon the fort at the approach of night, still kept up the firing. But in this they were mistaken, for instead of returning to the camp, the Americans still held their position, closing in gradually on the fort, in order to prevent the escape of any of the Moros during the ensuing night.

The commanding officer, seeing that they were determined to hold out until the bitter end, now issued orders for the construction of scaling ladders with which to gain admittance to the fort. Work was immediately begun on them but they were destined never to be used for that purpose at least, for about midnight the Moros, finding that we were still determined to hold our positions, decided to attempt an escape from the enclosure. The night was unusually dark, and the clouds were hanging low over the lake, rendering it almost impossible to see or distinguish an object at a greater distance than fifty feet. The Americans had anticipated their escape, and consequently were in constant readiness at all times during the night. Then suddenly a shot was heard which had been fired by some vigilant sentinel on guard, then another, and another.

It now became evident that they had charged the lines and were making a dash for liberty. In an instant every soldier was on the alert. They kept on coming, however, seemingly regardless of death or the rain of bullets. But few of them escaped or even lived to tell the tale, for as fast as they left the fort they were being shot down by a constant stream of fire from the Infantry, and when the morning dawned it was found that the Sultan of Maciu, with many another leader and tribesman, had fallen, never to breathe again.

During the struggle, the Sultan Cabugatan of Maciu, seeing that his efforts to suppress the Americans were in vain, rushed into camp, *bolo* in hand, in wild, frenzied excitement, determined to slay in cold blood everybody wearing an American uniform. But his savage intentions were brought to a speedy termination by the troops, who, on seeing him approach them, rushed towards him and overpowered him. However, he unfortunately succeeded in seriously wounding one of the best and bravest soldiers in the command, Private Richard G. Macbeth, of Co. "F" 27th U. S. Infantry, whose bravery in time of danger had made him an unanimous favourite among his comrades. Another victim of this savage Sultan was Pvt. James Nolan, Jr., of Co. "G" 27th U. S. Infantry, who, having been detailed as a scout, had fearlessly advanced upon one of the forts in order to secure, if possible, some information regarding their position and strength. He had reached the outer entrance when he met a storm of bullets from within, one of them hitting him in the right eye, inflicting a wound from which he suffered great pain.

But their sufferings were doubly avenged, for many a hitherto unconquerable Moro has fallen upon the green and now deserted territories of the Sultan of Maciu, with the bones of his mortal composition bleaching on the green sward, under the tropical sun of his native skies.

*Where once in triumph on his trackless plains*
*The haughty Moro Sultan loved to reign,*
*With shacks proportioned to his native sky,*
*Strength in his arm, and lightning in his eye,*
*He roamed with uncovered feet, his sun-illumined zone.*
*The dirk, the bolo, and the spear his own;*
*Or lead the combat wild without a plan*

*An artless savage, but a fearless man.*
*But his 'sun' of triumph, has set to rise no more*
*O'er the quiet waters of Lake Lanao's shores."*

It is now January 1, 1903, and the Moro campaign is drawn to a successful and favourable close, and "Old Glory" of fair "Columbia" is now unfurled to the gentle touch of the oriental zephyrs on the hill-tops of Mindanao, for all time to come.

THE TRUMPETER'S "LAST CALL" AT FORT MACIU.

*Bleeding, sore, and wounded, and by my foes surrounded,*
*The Trumpet once I sounded, no longer can be heard,*
*For it lies dust-stained and gory, and by the dust corroding,*
*Where once I blew melodious that call that cowards dread.*
*No longer in the battles will I call the boys to rally*
*Through dark ravines or valleys, for freedom and for right,*
*For my life's blood fast is flowing, and I am left alone*
*To die and to bemoan my fate at Maciu's fight.*
*"Stay, Comrade, do not leave me alone upon the field*
*Where the savage Moros wield their bolos and their spears,*
*For I may yet survive to see Maciu's tribe—*
*Like savage cowards—beat a long retreat."*
*Again I see in fancy the scenes in dear old Boston,*
*Where in childhood days I wondered free from care and strife;*
*The unforgotten homestead, surrounded by the foliage.*
*Where oft my welcomed footsteps have echoed through the night.*
*My last hour is approaching: death's dismal cloud is o'er me;*
*But being a true-blue soldier, I murmur not to die.*
*To-morrow's sun shall find me far from the skirmish line—*
*So to comrades left behind, I bid a long Good-bye.*

John J. Reidy

# The 27th Infantry

It is with feelings of pride and national patriotism we have watched through many a stormy year the steady growth and accomplishments of our immortal Army, whose splendid display of true valour and military discipline has attracted the attention and well-deserved admiration of all nations through the universe, whether exhibited on the expansive parade ground, under the balmy, azure blue skies of our Western Continent, of perpetual freedom, or on the far away "Eastern Isles," under the warm rays of the tropical sun, where many a true and stout-hearted son of "Fair Columbia" has sacrificed his young life for his country's cause. And as we look back to the long misty vale of tumbled years, in silent perusal and contemplation of the pages of our nation's history, we cannot help being for the moment awestruck, as we read from those cherished pages of the many bloody battles and more glorious victories, which have been won at all times, adown the ages, since first the cold, haughty invader sought to enter and deprive us of that freedom for which so many of our revered ancestors so nobly fought and died. But although those brave warriors of olden days have all passed away, and the regiments, by whose gallantry our "Stars and Stripes" was borne to victory, are now known to us only by name, yet we are more than proud to be able to acknowledge to the world, that they have been supplanted by regiments as noteworthy as ever faced in combat a mortal foe. And among them, and perhaps the most illustrious of them all, is the gallant 27th Infantry, whose distinguished achievements since its organization at Plattsburg, New York, and Fort McFerson, Ga., in the early part of the year 1901, are unexcelled and unequalled by any regiment that has been ordered forth in defence of our country and flag.

In December 1901, the 27th Regiment of U. S. Infantry was ordered from Plattsburg Barracks, N.Y., to proceed with all haste to Manila, P. I., and thence to the Island of Mindanao, to aid in suppressing and overthrowing the semi-civilized savages, whose defiant, inhuman, and brutal treatment of the American soldiers was in every sense appalling.

They arrived in Manila on February 3, 1902, and after encamping there for a few days, proceeded to the very centre of hostilities, which was at that time in the Island of Mindanao.

And since then the broad road to civilization has been opened to the hitherto savage Moro tribes, and chiefly by the brave officers and men of the 27th Regiment.

And in conclusion we can only say that the memories of the true, loyal, and ever dauntless heroes of this new, though historical regiment, who gave and sacrificed their lives in the defence of, and for the glory of, their country, shall be indelibly printed on the tablets of our memories adown the annals of time.

*John J. Reidy*

# The 25th Battery of Field Artillery

Under the Army Reorganization Bill, passed in 1900, provision was made for an increase in the number of Field Batteries, three of which were to be equipped entirely with mountain guns. These were to be known as the 14th, 25th, and 28th Batteries of Field Artillery. Two of these Batteries were to be organized in the Philippine Islands. These were the 14th and 25th, and were organized by equally dividing the number of members in what was formerly known as Light Battery "C" of the 7th Artillery. The two Batteries were given their authorized strength of 120 men each by transferring the additional number of men required from the Coast Artillery.

They were not organized, however, until Sept. 23, 1901. About one month later they were fully equipped as "Mountain Batteries," and on April 1, 1902, the 25th Battery, under command of Captain W. S. McNair, was ordered to the Island of Mindanao, where trouble with the Moros had long been expected.

The 25th Battery of Field Artillery is equipped with four guns, which are known as the Vickers–Maxim 75 mm. quick firing mountain guns.

This calibre, 75 mm., or 2.9 inches, will be seen to be a very little less than that of the field gun in use in our service viz., 3.2 inches, but the power of this gun is much less than that of the field gun, for the following reasons:

It is necessary to make a carriage and gun whose parts shall all be within suitable limits of weight for packing on mules. This limit, placed on the weight, limits the strength that can be obtained, and also the length of the gun itself. Therefore the amount of powder used in these guns is much less than the amount used in the field guns, and the velocity of the shot when it leaves the gun is much less (about one-half) than it is for the field gun. The Vickers-Maxim gun is mounted in a cradle which has on either side a cylinder of oil, through which the gun draws a plunger in recoiling, and by this device the force of the recoil is taken up gradually and the carriage does not run back several feet as it would otherwise do, so that it is at once ready to load and fire again after each discharge.

The loading of the piece is very simple. The gunner grasps a lever which he pulls around to the right, thereby bringing out the breech-block and withdrawing the empty cartridge shell last fired. The new round is pushed into the gun, the gunner moves the lever in the opposite direction, or to his left, and the gun is ready to fire.

When the gun is to be moved it is taken in parts for packing as follows: The gun itself, the cradle, the trail, and the wheels and axle, each of which is a load for one mule.

The men get expert at this manoeuvre, and pack up the guns at command in a period of a little less than one minute, while they unpack and set up the gun ready for action with greater speed, the record for the 25th Battery being 20 seconds.

This gun is provided with various kinds of projectiles, the ones usually carried being shell, shrapnel and canister, and are known as Krupp prepared ammunition, which can be used in the same manner as an ordinary rifle cartridge. The shrapnel for this, as well as all field guns, is the projectile mainly depended upon, and like all field guns, the main work for them is to fire at the personnel of the enemy.

It is a common error amongst military men and others not well versed in the use of Artillery, to suppose that a field gun is intended for the purpose of making breaches in walls.

The fallacy of this idea can be seen at once by making an examination of the projectiles, which will be found to contain only the quantity of powder which you could hold in the palm of your hand. The shells contain 10 ounces, the shrapnel 3, the canister a little more than 2. Thus it may be readily seen that the guns used by the 25th Battery are not such destructive engines of war after all, but to those who would doubt their effectiveness, we should simply say: "Go and witness them in action."

Enough has been said to give the reader a correct idea of what a "Mountain Battery" is, with the history of what is known as the 25th Battery of Field Artillery, and thereby the object of the writer has been accomplished.

*James Edgar Allen*

# The Mountain Battery

Dedicated to Captain W. S. McNair
and command

*The stout-hearted warriors who have fallen in battle*
*In defence of their country, its freedom to save,*
*Whose memory shall live and will ne'er be forgotten*
*Though long have they mouldered to dust in their graves,*
*Could they but look back from their graves of cold slumber,*
*Where in silence they are sleeping long ages away,*
*And see their successors, brave, bold, and undaunted,*
*Who have fought the proud Moros on Mindanao's plains.*
*For foremost in the ranks of victorious honour,*
*Are the heroes who founded the illustrious name*
*Of the 25th Battery, and one may well ponder,*
*On the name of its Commander, with world renown fame.*
*He has led with envious credit and valour,*
*Over many mountain trails, through swamp and ravines,*
*That same immortal "Battery," whose presence in battle*
*Made the wild Moros tremble, like cowards in fear.*
*The walls of Pandapatan's impregnable fortress,*
*Which withstood all assaults from invaders of old,*
*Went down like the leaves in a storm.*
*When "Fire!" was his order, brave and bold.*
*Even famed Bayan forts were shaken,*
*And crumbled to pieces, before him that day,*

*When he sent the projectiles in rapid succession*
*Against those giant walls, on the second of May.*
*Forts Maciu and Butig, whose histories were warlike,*
*By Lake Lanao's still waters defiantly did stand,*
*Until this brave Commander and his khaki-clad heroes*
*Blew them to fragments, all over the land.*
*In history's pages his name is recorded,*
*To be linked with the memory of the true and the brave,*
*Who for the honour and freedom of their glorious country,*
*Have fallen to slumber in numberless graves.*
*Nor must we forget the brave men he commanded,*
*Whose fearlessness, heroism, and unequalled might,*
*Is fresh in the memory of all Dattos and Sultans,*
*And the dark-coloured tribesmen of Mindanao's rugged heights.*
*For to them is attributed our success in battles,*
*That were fought with such glory and national pride,*
*In Mindanao's valleys and on forest-covered mountains,*
*Where countless Moro warriors fought and died.*

James Edgar Allen

LEONAUR

# ALSO FROM LEONAUR
## AVAILABLE IN SOFTCOVER OR HARDCOVER WITH DUST JACKET

**A HISTORY OF THE FRENCH & INDIAN WAR** *by Arthur G. Bradley*—The Seven Years War as it was fought in the New World has always fascinated students of military history—here is the story of that confrontation.

**WASHINGTON'S EARLY CAMPAIGNS** *by James Hadden*—The French Post Expedition, Great Meadows and Braddock's Defeat—including Braddock's Orderly Books.

**BOUQUET & THE OHIO INDIAN WAR** *by Cyrus Cort & William Smith*—Two Accounts of the Campaigns of 1763-1764: Bouquet's Campaigns by Cyrus Cort & The History of Bouquet's Expeditions by William Smith.

**NARRATIVES OF THE FRENCH & INDIAN WAR: 2** *by David Holden, Samuel Jenks, Lemuel Lyon, Mary Cochrane Rogers & Henry T. Blake*—Contains The Diary of Sergeant David Holden, Captain Samuel Jenks' Journal, The Journal of Lemuel Lyon, Journal of a French Officer at the Siege of Quebec, A Battle Fought on Snowshoes & The Battle of Lake George.

**NARRATIVES OF THE FRENCH & INDIAN WAR** *by Brown, Eastburn, Hawks & Putnam*—Ranger Brown's Narrative, The Adventures of Robert Eastburn, The Journal of Rufus Putnam—Provincial Infantry & Orderly Book and Journal of Major John Hawks on the Ticonderoga-Crown Point Campaign.

**THE 7TH (QUEEN'S OWN) HUSSARS: Volume 1: 1688-1792** *by C. R. B. Barrett*—As Dragoons During the Flanders Campaign, War of the Austrian Succession and the Seven Years War.

**INDIA'S FREE LANCES** *by H. G. Keene*—European Mercenary Commanders in Hindustan 1770-1820.

**THE BENGAL EUROPEAN REGIMENT** *by P. R. Innes*—An Elite Regiment of the Honourable East India Company 1756-1858.

**MUSKET & TOMAHAWK** *by Francis Parkman*—A Military History of the French & Indian War, 1753-1760.

**THE BLACK WATCH AT TICONDEROGA** *by Frederick B. Richards*—Campaigns in the French & Indian War.

**QUEEN'S RANGERS** *by Frederick B. Richards*—John Simcoe and his Rangers During the Revolutionary War for America.

LEONAUR

# ALSO FROM LEONAUR
## AVAILABLE IN SOFTCOVER OR HARDCOVER WITH DUST JACKET

**CAPTAIN COIGNET** *by Jean-Roch Coignet*—A Soldier of Napoleon's Imperial Guard from the Italian Campaign to Russia and Waterloo.

**HUSSAR ROCCA** *by Albert Jean Michel de Rocca*—A French cavalry officer's experiences of the Napoleonic Wars and his views on the Peninsular Campaigns against the Spanish, British And Guerilla Armies.

**MARINES TO 95TH (RIFLES)** *by Thomas Fernyhough*—The military experiences of Robert Fernyhough during the Napoleonic Wars.

**LIGHT BOB** *by Robert Blakeney*—The experiences of a young officer in H.M 28th & 36th regiments of the British Infantry during the Peninsular Campaign of the Napoleonic Wars 1804 - 1814.

**WITH WELLINGTON'S LIGHT CAVALRY** *by William Tomkinson*—The Experiences of an officer of the 16th Light Dragoons in the Peninsular and Waterloo campaigns of the Napoleonic Wars.

**SERGEANT BOURGOGNE** *by Adrien Bourgogne*—With Napoleon's Imperial Guard in the Russian Campaign and on the Retreat from Moscow 1812 - 13.

**SURTEES OF THE 95TH (RIFLES)** *by William Surtees*—A Soldier of the 95th (Rifles) in the Peninsular campaign of the Napoleonic Wars.

**SWORDS OF HONOUR** *by Henry Newbolt & Stanley L. Wood*—The Careers of Six Outstanding Officers from the Napoleonic Wars, the Wars for India and the American Civil War.

**ENSIGN BELL IN THE PENINSULAR WAR** *by George Bell*—The Experiences of a young British Soldier of the 34th Regiment 'The Cumberland Gentlemen' in the Napoleonic wars.

**HUSSAR IN WINTER** *by Alexander Gordon*—A British Cavalry Officer during the retreat to Corunna in the Peninsular campaign of the Napoleonic Wars.

**THE COMPLEAT RIFLEMAN HARRIS** *by Benjamin Harris as told to and transcribed by Captain Henry Curling, 52nd Regt. of Foot*—The adventures of a soldier of the 95th (Rifles) during the Peninsular Campaign of the Napoleonic Wars.

**THE ADVENTURES OF A LIGHT DRAGOON** *by George Farmer & G.R. Gleig*—A cavalryman during the Peninsular & Waterloo Campaigns, in captivity & at the siege of Bhurtpore, India.

LEONAUR

# ALSO FROM LEONAUR
## AVAILABLE IN SOFTCOVER OR HARDCOVER WITH DUST JACKET

**LIFE IN THE ARMY OF NORTHERN VIRGINIA** *by Carlton McCarthy*—The Observations of a Confederate Artilleryman of Cutshaw's Battalion During the American Civil War 1861-1865.

**HISTORY OF THE CAVALRY OF THE ARMY OF THE POTOMAC** *by Charles D. Rhodes*—Including Pope's Army of Virginia and the Cavalry Operations in West Virginia During the American Civil War.

**CAMP-FIRE AND COTTON-FIELD** *by Thomas W. Knox*—A New York Herald Correspondent's View of the American Civil War.

**SERGEANT STILLWELL** *by Leander Stillwell* —The Experiences of a Union Army Soldier of the 61st Illinois Infantry During the American Civil War.

**STONEWALL'S CANNONEER** *by Edward A. Moore*—Experiences with the Rockbridge Artillery, Confederate Army of Northern Virginia, During the American Civil War.

**THE SIXTH CORPS** *by George Stevens*—The Army of the Potomac, Union Army, During the American Civil War.

**THE RAILROAD RAIDERS** *by William Pittenger*—An Ohio Volunteers Recollections of the Andrews Raid to Disrupt the Confederate Railroad in Georgia During the American Civil War.

**CITIZEN SOLDIER** *by John Beatty*—An Account of the American Civil War by a Union Infantry Officer of Ohio Volunteers Who Became a Brigadier General.

**COX: PERSONAL RECOLLECTIONS OF THE CIVIL WAR--VOLUME 1** *by Jacob Dolson Cox*—West Virginia, Kanawha Valley, Gauley Bridge, Cotton Mountain, South Mountain, Antietam, the Morgan Raid & the East Tennessee Campaign.

**COX: PERSONAL RECOLLECTIONS OF THE CIVIL WAR--VOLUME 2** *by Jacob Dolson Cox*—Siege of Knoxville, East Tennessee, Atlanta Campaign, the Nashville Campaign & the North Carolina Campaign.

**KERSHAW'S BRIGADE VOLUME 1** *by D. Augustus Dickert*—Manassas, Seven Pines, Sharpsburg (Antietam), Fredricksburg, Chancellorsville, Gettysburg, Chickamauga, Chattanooga, Fort Sanders & Bean Station.

**KERSHAW'S BRIGADE VOLUME 2** *by D. Augustus Dickert*—At the wilderness, Cold Harbour, Petersburg, The Shenandoah Valley and Cedar Creek..

LEONAUR

# ALSO FROM LEONAUR
## AVAILABLE IN SOFTCOVER OR HARDCOVER WITH DUST JACKET

**FARAWAY CAMPAIGN** *by F. James*—Experiences of an Indian Army Cavalry Officer in Persia & Russia During the Great War.

**REVOLT IN THE DESERT** *by T. E. Lawrence*—An account of the experiences of one remarkable British officer's war from his own perspective.

**MACHINE-GUN SQUADRON** *by A. M. G.*—The 20th Machine Gunners from British Yeomanry Regiments in the Middle East Campaign of the First World War.

**A GUNNER'S CRUSADE** *by Antony Bluett*—The Campaign in the Desert, Palestine & Syria as Experienced by the Honourable Artillery Company During the Great War .

**DESPATCH RIDER** *by W. H. L. Watson*—The Experiences of a British Army Motorcycle Despatch Rider During the Opening Battles of the Great War in Europe.

**TIGERS ALONG THE TIGRIS** *by E. J. Thompson*—The Leicestershire Regiment in Mesopotamia During the First World War.

**HEARTS & DRAGONS** *by Charles R. M. F. Crutwell*—The 4th Royal Berkshire Regiment in France and Italy During the Great War, 1914-1918.

**INFANTRY BRIGADE: 1914** *by John Ward*—The Diary of a Commander of the 15th Infantry Brigade, 5th Division, British Army, During the Retreat from Mons.

**DOING OUR 'BIT'** *by Ian Hay*—Two Classic Accounts of the Men of Kitchener's 'New Army' During the Great War including *The First 100,000* & *All In It.*

**AN EYE IN THE STORM** *by Arthur Ruhl*—An American War Correspondent's Experiences of the First World War from the Western Front to Gallipoli-and Beyond.

**STAND & FALL** *by Joe Cassells*—With the Middlesex Regiment Against the Bolsheviks 1918-19.

**RIFLEMAN MACGILL'S WAR** *by Patrick MacGill*—A Soldier of the London Irish During the Great War in Europe including *The Amateur Army, The Red Horizon* & *The Great Push.*

**WITH THE GUNS** *by C. A. Rose & Hugh Dalton*—Two First Hand Accounts of British Gunners at War in Europe During World War 1- Three Years in France with the Guns and With the British Guns in Italy.

**THE BUSH WAR DOCTOR** *by Robert V. Dolbey*—The Experiences of a British Army Doctor During the East African Campaign of the First World War.

www.ingramcontent.com/pod-product-compliance
Lightning Source LLC
Chambersburg PA
CBHW021056090426
42738CB00006B/374